DRAMATIC USES OF
BIBLICAL ALLUSIONS IN
MARLOWE AND SHAKESPEARE

by James H. Sims

UNIVERSITY OF FLORIDA PRESS / GAINESVILLE, 1966

IN MEMORIAM

JAMES WILLARD SIMS

He was a man, take him for all in all,
I shall not look upon his like again.
                         Hamlet, I.ii.187-88

UNIVERSITY OF FLORIDA MONOGRAPHS

Humanities

No. 1: *Uncollected Letters of James Gates Percival,* edited by Harry R. Warfel

No. 2: *Leigh Hunt's Autobiography: The Earliest Sketches,* edited by Stephen F. Fogle

No. 3: *Pause Patterns in Elizabethan and Jacobean Drama,* by Ants Oras

No. 4: *Rhetoric and American Poetry of the Early National Period,* by Gordon E. Bigelow

No. 5: *The Background of The Princess Casamassima,* by W. H. Tilley

No. 6: *Indian Sculpture in the John and Mable Ringling Museum of Art,* by Roy C. Craven, Jr.

No. 7: *The Cestus. A Mask,* edited by Thomas B. Stroup

No. 8: *Tamburlaine, Part I, and Its Audience,* by Frank B. Fieler

No. 9: *The case of John Darrell: Minister and Exorcist,* by Corinne Holt Rickert

No. 10: *Reflections of the Civil War in Southern Humor,* by Wade H. Hall

No. 11: *Charles Dodgson, Semeiotician,* by Daniel F. Kirk

No. 12: *Three Middle English Religious Poems,* edited by R. H. Bowers

No. 13: *The Existentialism of Miguel de Unamuno,* by José Huertas-Jourda

No. 14: *Four Spiritual Crises in Mid-Century American Fiction,* by Robert Detweiler

No. 15: *Style and Society in German Literary Expressionism,* by Egbert Krispyn

No. 16: *The Reach of Art: A Study in the Prosody of Pope,* by Jacob H. Adler

No. 17: *Malraux, Sartre, and Aragon as Political Novelists,* by Catharine Savage

No. 18: *Las Guerras Carlistas y el Reinado Isabelino en la Obra de Ramón del Valle-Inclán,* por María Dolores Lado

No. 19: *Diderot's Vie de Sénèque: A Swan Song Revised,* by Douglas A. Bonneville

No. 20: *Blank Verse and Chronology in Milton,* by Ants Oras

No. 21: *Milton's Elisions,* by Robert O. Evans

No. 22: *Prayer in Sixteenth-Century England,* by Faye L. Kelly

No. 23: *The Strangers: The Tragic World of Tristan L'Hermite,* by Claude K. Abraham

No. 24: *Dramatic Uses of Biblical Allusion in Marlowe and Shakespeare,* by James H. Sims

PREFACE

Of the leading English translations of the Scriptures which preceded the Authorized Version of 1611—the Great Bible (also called Cranmer's Bible), the Genevan Bible, and the Bishops' Bible—the English Bible which seems to have been most familiar to the playwrights discussed in this study is the Bishops' of 1568, revised in 1572, although all of them show evidence of acquaintance with the popular Genevan version of 1560, which was of a handy quarto size printed in Roman letter. Of the dramatists discussed none would have had access to the King James, or Authorized, Version at the time the plays under consideration were composed; however, Thomas Heywood, *A Woman Kill'd With Kindness*, in its quarto version of 1617, agrees more in its Biblical quotations with the Authorized Version than with any of the earlier versions. Since my conclusions generally depend on verbal similarity rather than on exact verbal identity with any particular English translation, I do not claim to have finally determined which version each playwright used. However, an agreement between the wording of the plays and the wording of passages in the Bible has led me to make the following assignment of particular versions to particular playwrights: Marlowe, the Genevan version; Jonson, Chapman, and Marston, the Bishops' Bible; Shakespeare, the Bishops' Bible; Dekker, the Bishops' Bible; and Heywood, the Authorized Version. There are, of course, exceptions, and where the version used is other than that here listed, the exception is noted. I have retained the spelling of the various Bibles but have modernized the typography, omitting "y" for "i," "u" for "v," "i" for "j," using the more familiar letter "s," and replacing scribal abbreviations except for the ampersand.

Though it may account at times for a dramatist's phrasing of a Biblical allusion, I have not dealt with the direct influence of the Book of Common Prayer, since the ultimate referent is the Bible. Both the dramatists and their audiences were exposed constantly to the Bible via the Book of Common Prayer as well as by reading and hearing sermons directly from the Bible, and this exposure, rather than the influence of liturgical references, is relevant to this study. The Elizabethan lectionary of 1559 (practically identical with the second Book of Edward VI issued in 1552) prescribed systematic reading of the Bible according to the Bishops' version, though the Genevan was probably read in some churches.

Citations to Marlowe correspond to the text and line-numbering of C. F. Tucker Brooke's edition (London, 1925); to Shakespeare, the New Cambridge Edition of Neilson and Hill (New York, 1942); to other playwrights of the period, Brooke and Paradise, *English Drama 1580-1642* (Boston, 1933). The latter anthology was used merely as a convenience.

I am particularly indebted to Professor T. Walter Herbert, who originally suggested the subject, and Professors Ants Oras and Ernest William Talbert for their invaluable criticism and intellectual stimulation. Richmond Noble, *Shakespeare's Biblical Knowledge,* has been of great value. Noble's consideration of Shakespeare's use of the Bible is quite different from mine, since he hardly touches on dramatic effect; but his listing of liturgical and Biblical references and his bringing together of both Shakespearean and Biblical bibliographical information make his book an essential tool in completing a study of this subject. I am grateful to the libraries of the University of Florida, the University of North Carolina, Duke University, and Vanderbilt University for allowing me to use their books and services. I wish to thank both the Southeastern Institute of Medieval and Renaissance Studies and Austin Peay State College for research awards under which the final stages of this work were completed.

Parts of this study, in slightly different form, have appeared earlier. The section on Marlowe is an expanded and revised version of a paper read before the Southeastern Renaissance Conference at Chapel Hill in April, 1958; part of the section on Shakespeare's comedies appeared as a Tift College faculty monograph in June, 1960.

Most of all, I am grateful to Elizabeth, my wife, for the help and encouragement she always provides.

J. H. S.

Clarksville, Tennessee
March, 1966

CONTENTS

INTRODUCTION

A scientist has recently observed that a particular science, say chemistry, differs from philosophy (and, by extension, literature and the humanities generally) as a skyscraper under construction differs from a collection of diverse and disconnected mansions. The latter may be "impressive in their beauty of design and conception, but no one of them is recognized by all as *the* skyscraper of philosophy."[1] In the monolithic, many-floored "topless tower" imaged here uniform method predominates, individual contributors are nearly anonymous, and all can agree that this *is* science.

But one need not accept this either-or analogy; the mansions are not really so disconnected nor the skyscraper so monolithic. And in literature the greatest artists are those whose works are firmly rooted in, while emerging beyond, the work of earlier artists. This study suggests that Shakespeare learned and perfected techniques of his predecessors, especially Marlowe, in dramatic uses of Biblical allusion, building a new mansion, not disconnected but in design evolving out of and in execution surpassing earlier dramatists.

I have selected the plays of Marlowe and Shakespeare that exhibit clear patterns. Marlowe's Biblical allusions in plays other than *Faustus* and *The Jew of Malta* are negligible; in Shakespeare every play includes Biblical allusion, but I have excluded consideration of plays and passages that do not exhibit the patterns encompassed in this study.[2] The connections between Shakespeare's uses of Scripture and those of other playwrights cannot be deduced from external evidence, but the similarities seem too strong to be coincidental; a continuity from early English drama through Shakespeare is evident. The mansions are not disconnected.

The scientist's figure of disconnected mansions does, however, apply to much of the work done on Shakespeare's knowledge and use of the Bible; up to quite recent years each writer seemed to be

1. Walker, *The Nature of Scientific Thought*, p. vi. (Complete information on cited works is in the Bibliography.)
2. See Noble, *Shakespeare's Biblical Knowledge*, pp. 261 ff., for an index which may be used to discover other illustrations of the patterns discussed in this study.

attempting to build *the* skyscraper rather than to relate his insights and observations to those of earlier writers. Furthermore, even recent scholars have written as though no one before Shakespeare had made such allusions integral in the nexus of dramatic parts.[3]

Turning to consider the nineteenth and early twentieth century analyses of the Bible in Shakespeare, one finds such works as Eaton, *Shakspeare and the Bible,* Wordsworth, *Shakspeare's Knowledge and Use of the Bible,* Carter, *Shakespeare, Puritan and Recusant* and *Shakespeare and Holy Scripture,* Burgess, *The Bible in Shakspeare,* and Anders, *Shakespeare's Books.* Eaton's slim volume lists parallels with negligible commentary; his thesis (undemonstrated) is that Shakespeare and the Bible had become almost indistinguishable by the mid-nineteenth-century so that "Shakspeare perpetually reminds us of the Bible . . . by an elevation of thought and simplicity of diction which are not to be found elsewhere."[4] Bishop Wordsworth claims not to be "aware that the attempt made in this small volume has been anticipated in any other" and to have trusted solely to his own "complete perusal and study of our great poet . . . with the . . . motive of doing him a justice, which he has not yet fully received."[5] Carter's purpose in both books is to prove Shakespeare, as well as his father, a Puritan. In the second book he sets out to demonstrate that Shakespeare's Bible was the Genevan and that, therefore, he was a Puritan. Burgess quotes Eaton and others (A. H. Strong, *The Great Poets and Their Theology,* Charles Ellis, *The Christ in Shakspeare,* Frank C. Sharp, *Shakspeare and the Moral Life*) but acknowledges no debt. His work is long on polemics and short on scholarship; see, for example, his statement that it is "a fact established beyond doubt [that] Shakspeare was a sincere believer in the Bible . . . and in the doctrines taught therein," and his justification of his use of the King James Version on the grounds that the years of translation (1604 to 1611), together "with the five years that followed, were the greatest of Shakspeare's life, during which he wrote his greatest dramas."[6] Presumably Shakespeare had access to the Authorized Version in manuscript prior to 1611!

3. See Ribner, "Marlowe and Shakespeare"; this otherwise fine essay misses effects of classical allusions by Marlowe in *The Jew of Malta* and *I Tamburlaine,* effects similar to those both he and Shakespeare achieved in the use of the Bible. Ribner's essay is considered in more detail in Chapter 2.

4. Pages 12-13.

5. Pages ix-x.

6. Pages ix, xi.

2

Anders cites Wordsworth and J. B. Selkirk, *Bible Truths with Shakespearean Parallels,* adding a few parallels of his own; he notes much more influence of the Prayer Book than any of his predecessors.

A few works of the same period are notable for disclaiming indebtedness. Such are Pownall, *Shakspere Weighed in an Even Balance,* Bullock, *Shakspeare's Debt to the Bible,* Ackermann, *The Bible in Shakespeare,* and Coleman, *Shakespeare and the Bible.* Pownall "wishes to state that he has derived no assistance whatever from any similar work (if any such there be) on the same subject"; his purpose to offer a "small tribute, humble but hearty, of appreciation to the immortal Bard"[7] is, however, fulfilled in part by what appear to be borrowings from Eaton. Bullock credits J. B. [*sic;* James Brown?], *Bible Truths, with Shakspearian Parallels* (London, n.d.), with originally identifying "fifty or sixty of the passages given"[8] in his book. The illustrations justify his new volume. Ackermann reproduces large sections of Burgess's prefatory quoted material verbatim without credit.[9] Coleman quotes Burgess on occasion, but he uses material paraphrased from Burgess without documentation; Coleman's study, more than any other, claims a uniqueness of approach: "We believe we have detected Shakespeare's inner voice, inquiring, heaven inspired, sounding above even the beauty and humanity of his dramatic message." This mystical revelation comes to Coleman through strange media. Of Falstaff's "I lie, I am no counterfeit: to die is to be a counterfeit; for he is but the counterfeit of a man who hath not the life of a man; but to counterfeit dying, when a man thereby liveth, is to be no counterfeit, but the true and perfect image of life indeed" (*I Henry IV,* V.iv.115-20), Coleman says: "this unworldly wisdom . . . only illustrates again how the character, the plot, the context frequently have little immediate relation to the author's expression of his deeper philosophy."[10]

As for Marlowe's use of the Bible, it has been practically ignored —one may say altogether ignored as a source of Shakespeare's methods of using Scripture.

Only since Richmond Noble's careful analysis and tabulation of

7. Pages vi-viii.
8. Page 30.
9. Cf. pp. 66-31 and Burgess, pp vii-viii.
10. Pages vii, viii, 10.

Shakespeare's knowledge of the Bible, in 1935,[11] have studies like those of John Erskine Hankins and J. A. Bryant, Jr., been produced, studies which, explicitly related to and built upon other such studies, reveal coherent patterns of Biblical allusion in the dramaturgy of the playwright.[12] Prior to 1935 Biblical allusion was considered primarily as decorative ornamentation, as a clue to the religious persuasions of the man Shakespeare,[13] or as evidence of the Shakespearean canon's position next to the Holy Bible in power to instill Christian morality.

Noble furnished both the raw material and some hints for the brilliant insights of Hankins into Hamlet's character and motivation as well as into Claudius's and Ophelia's.[14] Elliott's work goes a step further, showing the relevance of some Biblical allusions to the interpretation an actor should give to the climactic scene in *Hamlet*.[15] Both Fredson Bowers and Bryant reveal the connection between

11. *Shakespeare's Biblical Knowledge;* this is the most thoroughgoing and scholarly work to date on Shakespeare and the Bible. Noble acknowledges the work of Wordsworth and Carter while rejecting some of their findings and interpretations. But Noble has not dealt with Shakespeare's dramatic uses of the Bible in anything approaching the thoroughness which Frye assigns to him in *Shakespeare and Christian Doctrine,* p. 130. Noble's random comments on dramatic use are valuable but neither thorough nor systematic. Fripp, *Shakespeare: Man and Artist,* footnotes Carter but probably did not know of Noble's work, since he does not mention it. His excellent condensed treatment of the pervasiveness in Shakespeare of Scriptural allusions and theme (I, 98-102, 357-58) indicates that had he turned his hand to a thorough survey of the Bible in Shakespeare he would have out-Nobled Noble. He also cites many Biblical references in individual plays.

12. The most significant works are Hankins, "Religion in *Hamlet:* the Bible," in *Character of Hamlet*; Elliott, *Scourge and Minister*; and Bryant, *Hippolyta's View.* Whitaker, *Shakespeare's Use of Learning,* states that "Shakespeare's use of Biblical references apparently reveals more about his dramatic technique than about his religious views" (p. 62) but does not pursue this line of thought, and his complete dependence upon Noble blinds him to effective uses Shakespeare made of this particular facet of his learning. He says that "in the first three comedies . . . no special dramatic effect can be achieved by quoting Scripture" (p. 83). See, however, the discussion below in Chapter 3 of the comedies, including two of the "first three." Other essays and articles appear in the notes and the Bibliography. Frye's book is not listed here because he deals with theology, not Biblical allusion, and because instead of building on earlier works, he seeks to discredit them and to erect a new edifice.

13. For a much more recent attempt see De Groot, *The Shakespeares and "The Old Faith,"* who merely repeats and occasionally disputes the findings of Wordsworth, Carter, Noble, and Fripp, with appropriate documentation; his discussion of Shakespeare's use of the Bible is confined to presenting evidence purporting to increase the possibility that Shakespeare was a Catholic.

14. Hankins, pp. 172-91.

15. Pages 122 ff.

Biblical allusion and thematic considerations in *Hamlet,* though with sharp disagreement;[16] and Bryant, in *Hippolyta's View,* perhaps overstates the case in making Shakespeare a thoroughgoing Biblical typologist. These modern scholars certainly yield more valuable insight into the Christian core of Shakespeare's vision than the moralizing eulogies of the nineteenth century. But none of them has recognized the patterns of Biblical allusion which Shakespeare drew from earlier writers, particularly Marlowe,[17] and perfected as his own. I have undertaken in the following pages to reveal some of these patterns.

16. Bowers, "Hamlet as Minister and Scourge"; Bryant, pp. 117 ff. Bowers, unlike Bryant, does not explicitly connect the words *minister* and *scourge* with the Bible, but the Christian tradition which he discusses is of course based on Scripture.

17. The one near-exception is Hankins. In the essay cited above and in another in the same volume, "Religion in *Hamlet:* Repentance," pp. 203-4, he has shown a clear relationship between the statements on repentance in Hooker, *Of the Laws of Ecclesiastical Polity,* and the repentance of both Marlowe's Faustus and Shakespeare's Claudius; however, on the further dimension of the relationship between these two playwrights in the use of Biblical allusion he does not comment.

1. EARLY AND MINOR
DRAMATISTS

The Bible and Biblical allusion have played an important part in English drama from its beginnings. The early tropes in the medieval church were acted with Biblical characters and dialogue,[1] and the later cycles from the Fall of Satan to Doomsday were Biblical in outline and general content, their intention being pastoral instruction in the cardinal points of Christian history and doctrine. Even after the plays became the province of the guilds and included much ribaldry (which apparently appealed to the religious as well as to the secular audience), the stories were still the great Bible stories, modified, often anachronistically, but Biblical and liturgical in origin and in main outline. With such a background it is not surprising that despite interest in classical models of comedy and tragedy, the Biblical influence, passed down from the cycles through the morality plays and the "hybrid" plays,[2] should be pervasive in much Renaissance drama. Though the rising tide of nationalism and secularism spawned historical chronicle plays and other stories, the Bible remained one of the dramatist's sure sources —perhaps the surest source—of dramatically effective allusion. Sometimes, as Tilley shows in *A Dictionary of Proverbs*,[3] a Scriptural phrase had become proverbial in the literature of 1500 to 1700, but dictionaries of the period indicate that the ultimate source was still recognized as the Bible. From command performances before the great families and the monarch to regular presentations at the theater, the playwright could depend upon the Bible, along with classical mythology, as a richly rewarding frame of reference. The appeal to memory might be made through the broad outlines of a Bible story, through fairly precise Biblical names and phrases, or

1. Hardison, *Christian Rite and Christian Drama in the Middle Ages,* argues that early drama did not grow out of the tropes; I am adopting the traditional view.

2. Spivack, *Shakespeare and the Allegory of Evil,* pp. 255-69, gives a description of, and examples from, these transitional plays, mostly Biblical in character and plot like the mysteries, but including abstract vices and virtues like the moralities.

3. Cf., the text, p. 12 (Margery Eyre's "All flesh is as grass"), and Tilley, F 359, citing I Pet. 1:24.

through continued reiteration of a Scriptural motif. However the appeal was made, the dramatist could gain more hearty laughs, more serious, often ironic, insights, and more emotional responses of all kinds by references to the Bible than to any other one book.

The dramatic effect was occasionally due as much to official sermons as to the Bible itself, since these homilies sometimes used humor to make a serious point. For example, in Sermon VI of the second volume of homilies, "Against Excess of Apparel," the Elizabethans heard the anecdote of the European artist who wished to portray all nationalities in their typical manner of dress. This he could easily do until he came to the Englishman, whose fashions in dress changed so constantly that the artist knew not how to portray him until he hit on the idea of painting the Englishman naked with a bolt of cloth under his arm.[4] That the Elizabethans originated neither humorous nor ironically reversed Scriptural references, however, may be demonstrated by examples from the Chester plays, a still popular cycle dating back to the early fourteenth century.[5]

The broad outline of a Bible story might acquire humorous details. In one of the Chester plays the audience is invited one moment to laugh at Joseph as an old man cuckolded by a young wife and to realize the next moment the miracle of the virgin birth with fresh vividness. Seeing Mary for the first time after an absence, Joseph cries out:

> Three monthes shee hase bene from me,
> Now hase shee gotten here, as I see,
> A greate bellye like to thee,
> Since shee went awaie;
> And myne it is not, be thou boulde,
> For I am bouth ould and could;
> These thirtie wynters, thoughe I woulde,
> I mighte not plea no leaie.

4. *Certain Sermons or Homilies*, p. 186. (Vol. 1, 1547, 12 sermons; vol. 2, 1563, 20; vol. 3, 1569, 1 in 6 parts; total 33.) Queen Elizabeth commanded that these sermons be read "Plainly and distinctly . . . in such order as they stand in the Book" every Sunday and Holy Day and that when the book had been completed, "the same be repeated and read again, in such like sort as was before prescribed" (Preface, n.p.). Instances of the use of Biblical texts with the interpretation given in the homilies are noted below.

5. Chambers, *The Mediaeval Stage*, II, 348 ff.; see, however, Salter, *Mediaeval Drama in Chester*, pp. 33-53, for a radically different dating, from 1377 as the earliest to the reign of Henry VIII as the latest.

But when an angel explains to Joseph that "The childe that shee shall beare, i-wysse,/ Of the Holye Ghoste begotten is" (cf. Matt. 1:20-25)[6] and the mood of the play suddenly shifts back to the serious contemplation of doctrinal truth, the momentary flash of fun has had its effect in heightening the wonder in the birth of Jesus.

Again, in his dying speech, the slaughtering King Herod paraphrases the words of the dying Christ.

> My legges rotten and my armes,
> I have done so manye harmes,
> That now I see of feindes swarmes,
> From hell cominge after me;
> I have done so moche woe,
> And never good seith I mighte goe,
> Therefore I see coming my foe,
> To feche me to hell.
> *I bequeath heare in this place*
> *My soule to be with Sathanas.*
> I dye nowe, alas! alas!
> I maie no longer dwelle.[7]

The italicized words (italics added) are in grim parody of Christ's "Father into thy hands I commend my spirit" (Luke 23:46).

Such allusions are continued in Elizabethan drama. The dramatists in the late sixteenth and early seventeenth centuries could be sure that their audiences would recognize and respond to Biblical allusions. Nonattendance at church was a punishable offense and the Bible was heard there regularly each week. The Bible was, moreover, the most widely translated, read, and discussed book of the age.[8]

There is little Biblical allusion in the plays of some Elizabethan-Jacobean playwrights,[9] and in others the dramatic usage is unre-

6. Wright, *The Chester Plays*, I, 98, 99.
7. Wright, I, 185-86.
8. See note 4, above, on *Certain Sermons*. An extremely well-written account, both interesting and amusing, of Elizabethan sermons, their preachers, and their audiences is Herr, *The Elizabethan Sermon*. Among other interesting facts, Herr describes how preaching at St. Mary's Hospital and Paul's Cross would be attended by five or six thousand people, attracted by both the preaching and such sideshows as penitents exposed to public jeers and gibes during the sermons (p. 24). Reports quoted by Herr indicate that the attitudes and responses of sermon-goers were not very different from those of playgoers.
9. For example, Beaumont and Fletcher use the Bible for humorous characterization and laughs in *The Knight of the Burning Pestle* and then limit their

markable. In *The Shoemakers' Holiday* Thomas Dekker used the
Bible primarily in the portrayal of humorous character; in *A Woman
Kill'd With Kindness* Thomas Heywood used it to aid in portraying
serious character; and in *Eastward Ho!* the Chapman-Jonson-
Marston collaboration used a Scriptural and a dramatic motif to
unify the action and to foreshadow the outcome. Since the uses of
the Bible made by these playwrights are quite simple and straightforward, a few passages from their plays will serve to introduce the
more complex and subtle practices of Marlowe and Shakespeare.

In *The Shoemakers' Holiday* Dekker portrays Margery Eyre so
that, though she quotes Scripture seriously, the audience is likely
to laugh at her. Fully as important to the character of Simon Eyre
as his favorite self-evaluation—"Prince am I none, yet am I princely
born"—is his frequent use of exotic names culled from the Bible
(as well as from other sources) as forms of address to his shoemakers: "mad Mesopotamians" (III.i.99), "mad Philistines"
(III.i.135), "Babylonian knaves" (III.iv.193), "mad Cappadocians"
(V.ii.57), and "fine dapper Assyrian lads" (V.ii.64). Simon is
acquainted with and (if one may judge by the spelling) correctly
pronounces Bible names. His wife, however, is more like the
grocer's wife in *The Knight of the Burning Pestle*, who mispro-
nounces Mulcaster's name and even refers to "Jone and the wall"
as a Bible story.

As her husband rises in the world, Margery seeks to rise to the
occasion in dress, speech, and manners. In Act III, Scene IV, "her
worship" is most fully presented as the wife who realizes her responsibility to "this world's calling." She is able to drop neither her
coarseness nor her favorite expression—"let that pass"—nor is she
able to gain the respect of Eyre's workmen. She almost manages to
add a higher tone to her speech, partly through the use of the Bible;
yet just when she is trying hard to command respect, she appears
even more vain, talkative, and flighty than ever. She asks Roger
how she would look in a French hood.

---

use almost entirely to making imagery and phrasing more striking (e.g., *Phi-
laster* and *The Maid's Tragedy*). In Fletcher, *The Island Princess,* I find only
two clearly identifiable Biblical allusions, in spite of the centrality of Quisara's
conversion to Christianity. Later Ford and Shirley use the Bible often (e.g., the
former to increase the bawdiness of Grausis in *The Broken Heart,* the latter in
The Cardinal to emphasize in the Duchess's speech the wickedness of the
cardinal). Selective checking of many playwrights, however, suggests that rich
veins of Biblical allusion in all Elizabethan-Jacobean drama are waiting for
some hardy prospector to stake out and mine them.

9

Hodge. [Aside] As a cat out of a pillory—
        Very well, I warrant you, mistress.
Wife.   Indeed, all flesh is as grass; and Roger,
        canst thou tell where I may buy a good hair?

                                        (III.iv.50-51)

The Scriptural phrase "all flesh is as grasse, and all the glorie of man is as the flower of grasse" (I Pet. 1:24) ill suits with her intense interest in dressing as befits her new station. That she is not thinking of the serious implications of the phrase is shown by her immediate question (arising from association between "grass" and "hair" perhaps) about acquiring a hair-piece to add to her "glory." Similarly, when she echoes "the wonderful workes of God" (Acts 2:11) with no spiritual understanding of the words, she is glibly rationalizing her wish to rise in society: "Fie upon it, how costly this world's calling is; perdy, but that it is one of the wonderful works of God, I would not deal with it" (III.iv.64-66).

When she first sees the returned veteran Rafe, Margery exclaims: "The left leg is not well; 't was a fair gift of God the infirmity took not hold a little higher, considering thou camest from France; but let that pass" (III.iv.88-91). This is the bawdy "powder-beaf-quean" of earlier in the play, but she has added to her suggestive comment the pious phrase " 't was a fair gift of God." Dekker probably meant her to allude to Paul's general discussion of marriage and celibacy: "For I wolde that all men were even as I my-selfe am: but everie man hathe his proper gift of God, one after this maner, and another after that" (I Cor. 7:7). Rafe's proper or "fair gift of God" was having escaped the French disease; in comparison, the losing of the power of a limb was not bad at all, according to Mrs. Eyre. When Rafe learns that Jane's whereabouts is not known, he begins to weep. Margery, touched with compassion, seeks to provide Scriptural consolation: "And so as I said—but, Rafe, why dost thou weep? Thou knowest that naked we came out of our mother's womb, and naked we must return; and, therefore, thank God for all things. . . . Alas, poor soul, he's overcome with sorrow; he does but as I do, weep for the loss of any good thing. But Rafe, get thee in, call for some meat and drink: thou shalt find me worshipful towards thee" (III.iv.124-28, 135-39).

Although one senses Margery's sympathy, the ludicrous image of returning to the mother's womb makes one laugh; before being conscious of the Christian acceptance of God's will involved in

10

thanking "God for all things" (Eph. 5:20) we are chuckling. The same image from the lips of Job gives rise to no laughter, partly because of the sober character of Job but also because of the verbal and spatial context of the image. "Then Job arose, and rent his garment, and shaved his head, and fel downe upon the grounde, and worshiped, and said, Naked came I out of my mothers wombe and naked shal I returne thether: the Lord hathe given and the Lord hathe taken it; blessed be the Name of the Lord" (Job 1:20-21). In the Biblical scene Job is lying on the ground; it is hither—to a grave in the earth—that he shall return. In Job's words the image conveys a sublime concept of human mortality; in Margery's it is amusing. But though Margery's misunderstanding is funny, it reminds us of the half-shocked, half-amused reaction of Nicodemus to Jesus's dictum "Ye must be borne againe": "How can a man be born when he is old? can he enter the seconde time into his mothers wombe, and be borne?" (John 3:4).

Like Dekker, Thomas Heywood used Biblical allusions and quotations to sharpen aspects of character. Though these are almost entirely in the speech of serious characters, in *A Woman Kill'd With Kindness* Heywood has Nick, quite in keeping with his humorous rhetoric, preface his decision on what song the servants should dance to with "It hath been, it now is, and it shall be." But a more characteristic example occurs in a serious context: when Nick informs Frankford of the affair between Anne and Wendoll, he uses the Old Testament phrase "make your ears to tingle" (III.ii.44; I Sam. 3:11, Jer. 19:3, II Kings 21:12).

Except for references to Wendoll as a Judas (III.ii.105-6; IV.v.39-41), Frankford is given two Biblical allusions, both of them in the same connection: his effort to disbelieve Nick's report of Anne's infidelity. When Nick has revealed to Frankford that Wendoll enjoys Anne and dishonors him, Frankford replies:

> What did'st thou say? If any word that touch'd
> His credit, or her reputation,
> It is as hard to enter my belief,
> As Dives into heaven. (III.ii.65-68)

A few lines later when Nick claims to have witnessed Anne's unfaithfulness, Frankford argues:

> Thy eyes may be deceiv'd, I tell thee;
> For should an angel from the heavens drop down,

11

And preach this to me that thyself hast told,
He should have much ado to win belief;
In both their loves I am so confident.   (III.ii.86-90)

Heywood has Frankford say that it would be hard for the charge against Anne and Wendoll to enter his belief: it would be "easier for a camel to go through the eye of a needle" (Matt. 19:23-24). In the second instance Frankford calls up the Pauline image of the necessity of rejecting falsehood even if preached by an angel from heaven: "But though that we, or an Angel from heaven, preache unto you otherwise then that which we have preached unto you, let him be accursed" (Gal. 1:8). Yet only ten lines after the angel image, Frankford is referring to Wendoll as the "Judas that hath borne my purse" and "sold me for a sin," and before the scene closes, Frankford is planning a trap for the two suspected lovers. Such speech, though conventional hyperbole, strengthens an interpretation of Frankford as a "false perceiver" of himself as well as of others.[10]

The Bible is quite differently used in *Eastward Ho!* Although the allusions in this play also provide insight into character,[11] Scripture here serves most strikingly as a motif to unify and foreshadow action, strengthening the development of a single theme. The Elizabethan playgoer would have known early how the play was going to end. In the opening scene appear both a faithful apprentice and a frivolous one. Touchstone gives the key to the story with allusion to Scripture, although the very names and attitudes of the two apprentices have already shaped the observer's attitude towards them. Calling to mind both the parable of the prodigal son (Luke 15) and the old tradition of school plays dramatizing the parable, Touchstone says to Quicksilver: "As for you, Master Quicksilver,

10. In "Honor and Perception in *A Woman Kill'd with Kindness*," Spacks sees the play not in the tradition of the homiletical object lesson in patience and forgiveness with Frankford as a paragon, but as a pessimistic play revealing Frankford as a "false perceiver" and the other main characters of both plots as "false objects of perception"; Nick is the only honorable character who is what he seems to be. Though hers is a modern reading of the play as a "unified, if somber, vision of a world largely governed by considerations other than honor" (p. 332), it agrees with the implications of Heywood's use of Biblical allusion in Frankford's speech.

11. For example, Touchstone's love of word play and his attitude towards his wife are highlighted by such obvious references as that to Matt. 10:38 in IV.ii.34-37; though his wife is the cross he has to bear, he will keep her to "fright away sprites."

think of husks,[12] for thy course is running directly to the Prodigal's hog's-trough. Husks, sirrah! Work upon that now" (I.i.127-30). When Quicksilver, having left Touchtone's shop, appears at Security's house, Security refers to Quicksilver's practice of reveling in "prodigal similitude" (II.ii.8), and the apprentice himself, upon removing his working clothes, says of his costume, "There lie, thou husk of my envassal'd state." It has already been made clear that Sindefy is Quicksilver's doxy, but a Scriptural allusion emphasizes the situation. Quicksilver says,

> I, Samson, now have burst the Philistine's bands;
> And in thy lap, my lovely Dalida,
> I'll lie and snore out my enfranchis'd state.   (II.ii.42-44)

Acquaintance with the story of Samson and Delilah in Judges 16 would indicate to the audience that Quicksilver, like Samson before him, is heading for a fall.

Golding, the faithful apprentice who remains at home like the good son in the Gospel of Luke (but who befriends the prodigal later, unlike the Gospel character), says to Quicksilver: "Go, thou most madly vain, whom nothing can recover but that which reclaims atheists, and makes great persons sometimes religious: calamity" (I.i.187-90). But it is the repetition of the prodigal theme which keeps the audience looking forward not only to the hog-trough but also to the happy ending. As already mentioned, Security refers to Quicksilver's fast living in "prodigal similitude" early in the play; after he has been caught by natural calamity and brought before the deputy (Golding himself), he is reminded of his master's substance which he has "prodigally consumed" (IV.ii.345); when he has repented and been converted in prison he says, like the prodigal of Scripture, when confronted by Touchstone, "O sir, I am not worthy to see your worshipful face!" (V.v.155, cf. Luke 15:19). At the end of the play Touchstone utters the key word "prodigal" again and adds the figure of the "lost sheep," also from Luke 15.

> Behold the careful father, thrifty son,
> The solemn deeds which each of us have done;
> The usurer punish'd, and from fall so steep
> The prodigal child reclaim'd, and the lost sheep.
>   (V.v.246-49)

12. "Husks" indicates either the Genevan or the Rheims version. The Bishops' Bible has "cods."

13

There are certainly other means used by the authors to unify the action of their hodgepodge of characters and events,[13] but the frequent reiteration of the prodigal motif forms a strong thread which ties the elements together.

13. A recurring allusion used for humorous purposes is Security's phrase "hunger and thirst." He certainly is not using it in the sense of Matt. 5:6, as a passion for righteousness; thus it is fitting that the suggestive phrase should recur in a toast to his wife as she is preparing to run off with Sir Petronel (III.iii.90-91).

2. MARLOWE

Christopher Marlowe makes a most effective and yet subtle dramatic use of Biblical allusion in *The Tragical History of the Life and Death of Doctor Faustus* and in *The Tragedy of the Rich Jew of Malta*. The reader's persistent consciousness, throughout these plays, that things are out of joint and even upsidedown can be explained on other grounds; but the effect of a reversal in the order of things—a reversal in which black is often shading into gray and even changing to white and back again—is most satisfactorily explained by an analysis of Marlowe's use of the Bible. As though he held his work up to a looking glass where all things are reversed and yet appear to be in normal perspective, the apparent level of meaning turns out, upon close observation, to be accompanied by a subtler level which is often exactly its reverse.

This particular technique Marlowe does not extensively employ elsewhere. Biblical allusions, though they do occur in both *Tamburlaine* and *Edward II*,[1] do not there form a consistent pattern. Even in *Doctor Faustus* and *The Jew of Malta* Marlowe achieves ironic reversals in other ways. For example, Mephistophilis, contrary to expectation, is more sensitive to the dangers of blasphemy than Faustus: he is terrified by Faustus's unholy demands (317-18) and is afraid of being exorcised by "bell, book, and candle" in the Pope's apartment (885-86). But Marlowe's most effective means of providing the rear-view-mirror glance at conventional ideas and beliefs is by the use and abuse of Scripture.[2]

1. Cf. e.g., *I Tamburlaine*, 464-66, with Matt. 13:38, 44, 46; *II Tamburlaine*, 2848-49, with I Sam. 15:20-23 and Num. 22-24; *Edward II*, 2579-80, with Judg. 9:8-15. (Marlowe citations are to line numbers in the Brooke edition.)
2. In "Marlowe and Shakespeare," pp. 41 ff., Ribner sees Marlowe's use of allusion as much less related to the scene in which it occurs than similar uses in Shakespeare. On the basis of such allusions in *The Jew of Malta* and *I Tamburlaine*, Ribner concludes that "So far as dramatic craftsmanship is concerned, it cannot really be said that Shakespeare's debt to Marlowe was extraordinary" and that "The one area in which Shakespeare seems to have learned much from Marlowe is that of historical drama" (p. 53). The analysis of Marlowe's use of Biblical allusion in this chapter demonstrates that whatever might

15

Three types of reversal appear: the reversal of roles, the reversal of values, and the reversal of meaning. Analysis of certain passages will clarify these terms. To be sure, Marlowe like the dramatists already mentioned makes straightforward use of Biblical allusion, as in most of the speeches of the Old Man in *Doctor Faustus*.[3] But more characteristic and more effective are his reversals.

Reversal of roles occurs when words spoken by or of a righteous person (usually Christ) in the Bible are associated in the play with a wicked person (Mephistophilis, Faustus, and Barabas especially). The effect is shocking—much more shocking, for example, than the anti-papist device of dressing Mephistophilis in the habit of a Franciscan friar. Granted, the full significance would come only to those capable of recognizing the context of the allusion. Yet even those unread in the Bible heard Scripture every Sunday. At any rate the references, particularly in *Doctor Faustus*, suggest passages that would have been unknown to very few Elizabethan playgoers. The reversal of roles, therefore, though the audience in many instances may not have consciously analyzed what was wrong, could hardly have failed to produce a sharp sense of something badly out of frame.

When Mephistophilis promises Faustus, "And I wil be thy slave and wait on thee,/ And give thee more than thou hast wit to aske"

---

be said of classical allusion, his Biblical allusions cannot be called "pure decoration, unrelated . . . to the substance of the scene"; furthermore, Shakespeare's ironic use of the Bible in tragedy, as discussed below, seems clearly to have been learned from Marlowe and improved upon. In the light of Marlowe's ironic uses of the Bible, the examples Ribner cites of unrelated and even distracting classical allusion can be read as directly related and enlightening ironic reversals. Thus Ithamore's allusion to himself as Adonis and to Bellamira as Venus are probably intended to be ludicrous; Mycetes's charge to Theridamas to conquer Tamburlaine "As did Sir Paris with the Grecian dame" both intensifies Mycetes's bumbling stupidity and foreshadows Tamburlaine's verbal rape by which Theridamas is robbed of loyalty to Mycetes. Considered in this light, the allusion also suggests that the real rapist was Helen, not Paris, since the hunter becomes the caught. In short, Marlowe's use of allusion seems to me dramatically effective and Shakespeare's seems to have developed from Marlowe's.

3. See Wilson, *Marlowe and the Early Shakespeare*, pp. 70-74, for a concise summary of W. W. Greg's solution of the play's textual problems in *Marlowe's 'Doctor Faustus' 1604-1616 Parallel Texts* (1950) and *The Tragical History of the Life and Death of Doctor Faustus: A Conjectural Reconstruction* (1950). If Marlowe's collaborator wrote the Old Man scenes, as Wilson says (p. 80), the more commonplace uses of Biblical allusion in the play are not Marlowe's. For a critical review of Greg's *Parallel Texts*, see Fredson Bowers, "The Text of Marlowe's *Faustus*," *MP*, XLIX (1952), 195-204.

16

(478-79), the audience is reminded of the passage, "Now unto him therefore that is able to do exceeding abundantly above all that we aske or thinke . . . Be praise" (Eph. 3:20-21a) and is brought up short. A devil ascribes to himself a power that the Bible ascribes to God; Marlowe presents a world of theological and moral ideas seen in reverse as through a looking glass. This is in accord with the quest of Faustus, who, believing that he cannot get what he wants from God through the study of divinity, aims to satisfy his lusts through recourse to Lucifer.

Dr. Faustus even becomes a kind of perverted Christ who sheds his blood not to save the souls of others but to damn his own soul and then appropriates the death cry of the Biblical Christ to emphasize the blasphemy. As Faustus prepares to write a quit-claim deed to his soul with his own blood, he says, "View heere the blood that trickles from mine arme,/ And let it be propitious for my wish" (489-90). Paul said of Christ: "Whome God hathe set forthe to be a propitiation through faith in his blood" (Rom. 3:25);[4] but Faustus thinks of his blood as being propitious in his suit to Lucifer. Then he exclaims,"*Consummatum est,* this Bill is ended" (506), as an echo of Christ's "It is finished" (John 19:30).[5] According to traditional Christian theology, these words were a cry not of defeat but of triumph that the work of redemption by the blood of Christ was completed and that now the souls of men could be freed from Hell. On Faustus's lips, however, the words became a grim statement of a diametrically opposed transaction: by his own blood Faustus seals his own soul's condemnation. The Scriptural language used makes a horrifying situation more horrible by adding a blasphemous parody of holy utterances, an element associated by the

4. This quotation is from the Bishops' Bible. The Genevan, followed in all other quotations from Marlowe, has "Reconciliation" in Rom. 3:25 instead of "propitiation."

5. See Hunter, "The Theology of *The Jew of Malta.*" As far as I can determine, Hunter is the first to note in print the striking similarities between Marlowe's technique of allusion in *Faustus* and *The Jew.* Of Faustus's use of *consummatum est* Hunter says, "we see *round* his self-assertion into the Order that it breaks, even at the moment when it breaks it" (p. 211). Hunter's article is a model of convincing analysis based on a close reading of the text against a background of impressively marshaled external evidence. In addition to noting some of Barabas's reversals of Biblical quotation, Hunter emphasizes a further dimension in the audience's probable reaction to Barabas as a representative of the race now cut off from God's promises to Abraham, promises that apply to Abraham's children by faith (Christians) and not to his ethnic descendants without faith. See other notes to Hunter below.

17

Elizabethans with such whispered-about abominations as the Black Mass.

There are similar examples in *The Jew of Malta*; here Marlowe reverses roles between Barabas and Job, and even more shocking in some ways than the reversal in *Faustus*, between Barabas and Christ. When, in the tradition of Job's "friends," the "friends" of Barabas gather around after the Governor of Malta has seized all his known wealth, one of them urges him to "remember Job."[6] Barabas replies, "I had

> As much as would have bought his beasts and him,
> And yet have kept enough to live upon;
> So that not he, but I may curse the day,
> Thy fatall birth-day, forlorne *Barabas*;
> And henceforth wish for an eternale night,
> That clouds of darkenesse may inclose my flesh,
> And hide these extreme sorrowes from mine eyes:
> For onely I have toil'd to inherit here
> The months of vanity and loss of time,
> And painful nights have been appointed me.   (422-31)

Barabas is quoting and paraphrasing from the third and seventh chapters of the Book of Job. "After this opened Job his mouth, and cursed his day. . . . Let darknesse and the shadowe of death stain it; let a cloud dwell upon it; let the blacknesse of the day terrifie it. . . . [Curse the night of my conception] because it shut not up the doores of my mothers wombe, nor hid sorrow from mine eyes. . . . So am I made to possess monthes of vanity, and wearisome nights are appointed unto me" (Job 3:1, 5, 10; 7:3). Barabas, by claiming to be in far worse straits than Job ever was, intensifies his own hypocrisy, for Barabas has enough cash hidden away to start getting rich all over again, a fact revealed immediately after this lamentation. Thus what sympathy one may have felt for Barabas begins to slip away, and by the time he has persuaded Abigail to feign conversion to Christianity in order to regain his hidden gold from the nunnery, any identification with him is gone, though much worse hypocrisies lie ahead.

A Biblical allusion casts Barabas in Christ's role early in the play. Depriving Barabas of all his wealth to pay tribute as protection against Turkish attack, the Christian Governor of Malta says:

6. See Hunter's discussion of Barabas as an "Anti-Job" and even an "Antichrist," pp. 219-20, 233-34.

18

No, Jew, we take particularly thine
To save the ruine of a multitude;
And better one want for a common good
Then many perish for a private man.   (329-32)

Marlowe calls to mind the meeting of another council in which the
presiding officer argued that it was better for one to suffer for the
sake of all. The Jewish high priest Caiaphas, discussing before the
Sanhedrin the possibility that the Romans might punish all the Jews
because of the Messianic claims of Jesus, said: "It is expedient for
us, that one man should die for the people, and that the whole
nacion perish not" (John 11:50). Here is a looking-glass view indeed: the Jewish high priest becomes the Christian governor of
Malta, and the founder of Christianity, a Jew himself of course,
becomes the rich Jew Barabas, named for the criminal released by
Pilate instead of Jesus. The dialogue which immediately follows
maintains the reversed order of things and intensifies it.

1 Knight. If your first curse fall heavy on thy head,
            And make thee poore and scorn'd of all the world,
            'Tis not our fault, but thy inherent sinne.
Barabas. What?, bring you Scripture to confirm your wrongs?
        .   .   .   .
            But say the Tribe that I descended of
            Were all in generall cast away for sinne,
            Shall I be tried by their transgressions?
            The man that dealeth righteously shall live:
            And which of you can charge me otherwise?[7]
                                    (340-43, 346-50)

In answer to the knight's references to the curse of God upon dis-
obedient Jews (seen in such passages as Ps. 44:13, Deut. 28:15, and
Mal. 2:20), Barabas self-righteously identifies himself with a passage in Isaiah often regarded as a Messianic prophecy. "He that
walketh in justice, and speaketh righteous things, refusing gaine of
oppressions, shaking his hands from holding of bribes, stopping his
eares from hearing of blood, and shutting his eyes from seeing of
evil; he shal dwell on high" (Isa. 33:15-16a). Although at this point
in the play Barabas has not been revealed in his full wickedness,

7. In connection with this speech, Hunter (pp. 237-38) quotes a gloss on
Romans 11 from the Genevan Bible. While I do not deny the possibility of
Marlowe's intention to allude to this Scripture and its gloss, I consider of pri-
mary significance those Bible verses cited in my text above.

Machiavel's prologue,[8] soon to be confirmed by the action, has given a far less exalted description. But, more important, the question which Barabas asks at the close of the speech (350) paraphrases Christ's words to the Pharisees: "Whiche of you can rebuke me of sinne?" (John 8:46). Barabas implies that the doctrine of man's depravity does not apply to him as it did not apply to Christ. Such use of Biblical allusions to make black white and white black gives the audience a fresh perspective, a shaking-up that will jolt them into seeing, behind things as they purport to be, things as they really are. In *The Jew* Marlowe breaks down the distinctions traditionally imagined among Jews, Christians, and Turks (Mohammedans) so that all these groups may be seen as made up of individuals good and bad—but mostly as bad as the devil could wish. Who is most wicked seems to depend upon who has control.

A second type of Biblical allusion in Marlowe reverses values. Marlowe often uses such reversals without Biblical allusion, as when Faustus speaks of divinity, traditionally the most exalted of studies, as "basest of the three,/ Unpleasant, harsh, contemptible, and vilde" (136-37). But, as in the case of the reversal of roles, a wicked act or a blasphemous sentence appears even blacker if it involves abuse of Scripture. Before Faustus has signed away his soul, he sits alone in his study awaiting Mephistophilis, vacillating between a desire for salvation and a lust for all that magic can bring him, and deliberately he attempts to reverse his standard of values. For hope and faith in God, he would substitute "Despair in God, and trust in Belzebub," and he seeks to make firm his wavering purpose by making blasphemous avowals of what he will do for the devil. "The God thou servest is thine owne appetite,/ Wherein is fixd the love of Belzabub" (443-44). Faustus, Doctor of Divinity now turned necromancer, has found support for his new creed in the New Testament: "For they that are such [heretics] serve not the Lord Jesus Christ, but their owne bellie . . . whose end is damnacion, whose God is their bellie, and whose glorie is in their shame, whiche mind earthlie things" (Rom. 16:18; Phil. 3:19). Here Paul describes those who have exactly reversed Christian values: for the spirit, the belly; for heaven, damnation; for God and

8. See Meyer, *Machiavelli and the Elizabethan Drama*, pp. 30 ff. Marlowe was the first to introduce the Florentine on the stage; his Machiavel, an incarnate devil in the style established by Innocent Gentillet, is the prototype of such characters in Elizabethan-Jacobean drama.

his Son, their own appetites; for glory, shame. This credo Faustus struggles to adopt as his own, but he never entirely succeeds in substituting his appetite for his belief in "God that made the world" (686; Acts 17:24).

In *The Jew of Malta* Barabas undergoes no spiritual struggles over the reversal of values; he seems at ease with values already reversed. The contradictions between the Bible passages to which he alludes and the immoral code of revenge he is following are beyond his ken. As he says, "It's no sinne to deceive a Christian" (1074). Therefore when he has persuaded Abigail to fake a conversion to Christianity so that she may gain entry to his confiscated house, now a nunnery, to recover his hidden gold, Barabas feels justified in praying to God for guidance.

> O Thou that with a fiery piller led'st
> The sonnes of *Israel* through the dismall shades,
> Light Abrahams off-spring; and direct the hand
> Of Abigall this night. (651-54)

The reference is to Exodus 13:21. The fiery pillar of supernatural origin by which God led the Israelites from slavery under the Egyptians, whom they indeed robbed, is represented by a lantern in the hand of a Jew intent on filching gold from a Christian house. Marlowe is of course satirical toward Christians, but to Christian eyes the God of Abraham, who promised blessing to all nations through Abraham's offspring, is a stranger to the God of Barabas.[9]

After Barabas has regained his place as the richest man in Malta with a house as great and fair as the governor's, he can devote all his time to plotting revenge on the Christians in general and the governor in particular. When Lodowick, the governor's son, by his interest in Abigail, brings events to pass which will make it possible for Barabas to cause Lodowick's death, Barabas says, in an aside:

> Now will I shew myselfe
> To have more of the Serpent than the Dove;
> That is,—more knave than foole. (796-98)

The words of Jesus are perverted so that both the serpent and the dove figure become, in Barabas's words, symbols of something bad. When Jesus said to his disciples, "Beholde I send you forth as shepe in the middes of wolves: be ye therefore wise as serpentes, and

9. See Hunter, pp. 216-18.

21

innocent as doves" (Matt. 10:16), he intended the serpent and the dove as figures of two qualities, different but both good, to be balanced by Christians as they faced the hostility of the world (the "wolves"). To Barabas, schooled in the Machiavellian art of dissimulation, it seems better to be wickedly wise than innocently (in the sense of "harmlessly") foolish. To him the advice to be both wise and harmless is nonsense. He who has been seen, through the Marlovian looking glass of Biblical allusion, as a Christ figure now plans to carry out his fiendish schemes in accord with his version of an injunction of Christ.

To bring about the murder of Lodowick, Barabas encourages the young man in his desire for the beautiful Abigail.[10] A hint of the fate of Abigail is involved in the classical allusion Barabas makes when of Abigail, he says "I hold as deare/ As *Agamemnon* did his *Iphigen*" (175-76). An even clearer foreshadowing includes a Biblical allusion. When Lodowick asks if Barabas might help him obtain a diamond, Barabas replies:

O, Sir, your father had my Diamonds.
Yet I have one left that will serve your turne:—
[Aside] I meane my daughter: but e're he shall have her
I'le sacrifice her on a pile of wood.   (810-13)

He alludes to the offering up of Isaac, Abraham's only son. "When they came to the place whiche God had shewed him, Abraham builded an altar there, & laid the wood, and bound Izhak his son, and laied him on the altar upon the wood" (Gen. 22:9). Isaac's life was spared and Abigail's is not; the important differences, however, concern the motivations of Abraham and Barabas. Abraham's was an act of faithful obedience to God's command and of spiritual devotion to God. For the moral value of love of God superseding the love of child, Barabas substitutes love of hate and revenge superseding the love of child. A villain who accompanies his villainy by allusion to Holy Writ in which he has reversed the values, substituting natural scheming for supernatural providence, knavery for wisdom, and blind obedience to impulses of hate for obedience to God becomes, especially to an audience acquainted with the Scriptures, the child of Hell. And the state of one like

10. Abigail has the name and character of the attractive wife of the churlish Nabal who was smitten dead by God. Unlike Marlowe's Abigail, the Biblical heroine enjoyed a happy ending as the bride of David (I Sam. 25).

In *The Two Gentlemen of Verona* a scene which could hardly be other than hilarious is made even funnier by Launce's incorrect allusions to well-known Bible stories. As Launce soliloquizes on his departure for Milan with his master Proteus, he says: "I have receiv'd my proportion, like the prodigious son. . . . Now come I to my father: 'Father, your blessing.' Now should not the shoe speak a word for weeping" (II.iii.3-4, 25-26). Immediately after identifying himself with the "prodigious son," Launce takes off both shoes and uses them to personate his mother and his father; then he becomes Esau begging for the blessing of Isaac. Later, in conversation with Speed, Valentine's man, Launce identifies himself with Jesus.

Speed. But tell me true, will't be a match?
Launce. Ask my dog. If he say ay, it will; if he say, no,
it will; if he shake his tail and say nothing, it
will.
Speed. The conclusion is then it will.
Launce. Thou shalt never get such a secret from me but by
a parable. (II.v.35-41)

Matthew spoke of Jesus as one who talked "unto the multitude in parables; and without a parable spake he not unto them" (Matt. 13:34), and applied to Jesus the Old Testament phrophecy, "I will open my mouth in parables; I will utter things whiche have been kept secret from the foundation of the world" (Matt. 13:35). The incongruity is intensified when, a moment later, Launce shows that he considers the distinguishing mark of a Christian to be a willingness to drink ale with another Christian; if Speed will not go to the alehouse, he is "an Hebrew, a Jew, and not worth the name of a Christian" (II.v.57-58).[6]

In *Love's Labour's Lost* Don Armado, feeling a desire for Jaquenetta and wishing authoritative precedent for his love, asks Moth to remind him of some great men, "men of good repute and carriage," who have been in love. Moth replies, "Samson, master. He was a man of good carriage, great carriage, for he carried the town gates on his back like a porter; and he was in love" (I.ii.73-75). Moth's reference to Judges 16:3 is followed by a discussion of

6. For an interesting discussion of the clowns, and even of the dog, as structurally and thematically parallel to the main plot, see Brooks, "Two Clowns in a Comedy." The allusions noted above seem particularly significant to Brooks's discussion of this same passage (II.iii through II.vi), strengthening his contention that the clowns are organically a part of the play's theme.

31

> *Jerome's* Bible, *Faustus*, view it well.
> *Stipendium peccati mors est*: ha!, *Stipendium &c.*
> "The reward of sinne is death: thats hard.
> *Si pecassi negamus, fallimur, & nulla est in nobis*
> *veritas.*
> "If we say that we have no sinne, we deceive our selves,
> and theres no truth in us.
> Why then belike
> We must sinne, and so consequently die.
> I, we must die an everlasting death:
> What doctrine call you this, *Che sera, sera,*
> "What wil be, shall be?" Divinitye, adieu.   (66-75)

The first passage Faustus reads is the first half of Romans 6:23; the full verse is: "For the wages of sin is death; but the gift of God is eternal life through Jesus Christ our Lord." In the second passage, Faustus reads the first full sentence, but not the one which follows: "If we say that we have no sinne, we deceive ourselves, and trueth is not in us. If we acknowledge our sinnes, he is faithful and just to forgive us our sins, & to cleanse us from all unrighteousnes" (I John 1:8-9).

The original meaning—that although men are sinners doomed to death, a way of escape from that doom has been provided in Jesus Christ—is reversed and a fatalistic doctrine is falsely drawn from the Bible.[13] Even Faustus's reaction—"That's hard"—and his adieu to divinity are based on the New Testament story of those who turned back from discipleship when they decided that the doctrine of Jesus was too hard (John 6:60, 66). Directed by Mephistophilis (Appendix, 1424-28), Faustus deliberately reverses the meaning of the passages he reads because he is ravished with a desire for the intellectual and physical power that can be his through making the spirits his subjects; determined to close his eyes against the light, at the same time he wishes to blame his determination on fate. His set purpose to view himself as irrevocably damned in spite of his references to passages containing the promises of God's grace and

---

13. I noted this perversion of Scripture in a paper read before the Southeastern Renaissance Conference at Chapel Hill in 1958. Although it is fairly obvious to one familiar with the Bible, as far as I can determine the first printed comment on Faustus's reversal here is in Cole, pp. 198-199. Ribner has subsequently noted the same faulty syllogism in "Marlowe and Shakespeare," p. 49. See also Hunter, pp. 212-13; Hunter also points out the parallel to Despair's arguments to Spenser's Red Cross Knight.

24

forgiveness is made even more evident when he writes a deed to
bequeath his soul to Lucifer.

> *Consummatum est,* this Bill is ended,
> And Faustus hath bequeath'd his soule to *Lucifer.*
> But what is this inscription on mine arme?
> *Home fuge,* Whither should I flye?
> If unto God hee'le throwe me downe to hell . . .
>
> (506-10)

The question "Whither should I flye?" echoes the cry of the psalmist: "Whether shal I go from thy Spirit? Or whether shal I flee
from thy presence? If I ascend up into heaven thou art there; if I
lie downe in hel, thou art there. Let me take the wings of the
morning, and dwell in the uttermost partes of the sea; yet thether
shal thine hand lead me, & thy right hand holde me" (Ps. 139:7-10).
The reversal of meaning involved in the words of Faustus impugns
the willingness of God to receive those who come to him. The question of the psalmist implies the answer that there is no place where
the love and direction of God will be denied him; the question of
Faustus implies his belief that wherever he might flee, condemnation is sure. The psalmist believes God will be with him even in
Hell; Faustus believes God will reject him even from Heaven. Such
use of Biblical allusions by Faustus increases the tragedy of his end,
for in one as accomplished in the study of divinity as he, reversals
of meaning can only be deliberate, springing from his desire to gain
power and wealth through a pact with the devil and from his consequent need to consider himself already damned anyway. The
tragedy of Faustus is the tragedy of a man who perversely rejects
every proffered means of redemption through a desperate conviction, self-imposed, that he cannot repent and that even if he could
God would not save him.[14]

Yet there is an inner struggle as Faustus seeks to find some glim-
mer of hope for salvation in spite of his soul's having been signed

14. Campbell, *"Doctor Faustus:* A Case of Conscience": "Viewing Faustus
not as one whose fate was determined by his initial sin [of abjuring God] but
rather as one who until the fatal eleventh hour might have been redeemed,
we can account for the suspense which the play creates" (p. 239). Campbell
shows striking parallels between the structure and content of Marlowe's play
and the celebrated case of Francesco Spiera (anglicized to Francis Spira),
whose sufferings of conscience over having renounced his faith and given in
to despair were recorded by four distinguished scholars and issued as a book
prefaced by John Calvin in 1549 (p. 229).

Dro. S. Marry, sir, she's the kitchen wench and all
grease. . . . If she lives till doomsday, she'll
burn a week longer than the whole world.

Ant. S. What complexion is she of?

Dro. S. Swart, like my shoe, but her face nothing like so
clean kept: for why, she sweats; a man may go over
shoes in the grime of it.

Ant. S. That's a fault that water will mend.

Dro. S. No, sir, 'tis in grain; Noah's flood could not
do it.   (III.ii.96, 100-109)

Both past and future catastrophes are mentioned in the same New
Testament passage: "the world that then was, being overflowed
with water, but the heavens and the earth . . . are kept in store,
reserved unto fire" (IIPet. 3:6-7).

Noah's flood is alluded to in *As You Like It.* Jaques compares the
lovers promising faith to one another (Orlando-Rosalind, Oliver-
Celia, Silvius-Phebe) to Noah's couples of beasts coming to the
ark and Touchstone and Audrey to a pair of strange animals. "There
is, sure, another flood toward, and these couples are coming to the
Ark. Here comes a pair of very strange beasts, which in all tongues
are called fools" (V.iv.35-38). The allusion is to God's command
to Noah to take "of uncleane beasts by couples, the male and his
female" (Gen. 7:2).[8] This wry comparison by the melancholy
Jaques, who deliberately takes a cynical view of affairs—he will,
instead of lamenting them as was common, "rail against all the
firstborn of Egypt" (II.v.63-64)—brings laughter because of its
implied insistence on the reproductive purpose of marriage and its
highlighting of the strange courtship of Touchstone and Audrey.

A Biblical phrase used in Elizabethan times to mean "taken in
the act," often with suggestions of the sexual act, was "taken with
the manner." The Old Testament gives instructions on how to discover a wife's adultery when "there be no witnesse against her,
neither she be taken with the manner" (Num. 5:13). Thus when
Costard, in *Love's Labour's Lost,* says "The matter is to me, sir, as
concerning Jaquenetta./ The manner of it is, I was taken with the
manner" (I.i.204-5), the familiar expression invites a laugh and

8. Shakespeare used the Genevan version here instead of the more frequently used Bishops' Bible, which for "beasts" has "cattel" and for "couples,"
"two."

34

and, with one possible exception, all of his statements are Biblically phrased presentations of the orthodox Christian view of Faustus and the jeopardy in which he has placed his soul. One image used in the Old Man's exhortation to Faustus to repent and be saved indicates, perhaps, Marlowe's intention to raise a question not about the validity of the advice given, but about the possibility of its being accepted. The Old Man says,

> I see an Angell hovers ore thy head,
> And with a violl full of precious grace,
> Offers to powre the same into thy soule,
> Then call for mercye and avoid despaire.   (1291-94)

The image is Biblical, but the significance in the source is the reverse of that in the Old Man's speech. "And I heard a great voice out of the temple saying to the seven angels, Goe your wayes, and pour out the vials of the wrath of God upon the earth" (Rev. 16:1). The pouring out of these vials of God's wrath is followed by noisome sores, the seas and springs turning into blood, the scorching of men with the heat of the sun, and other such plagues. Although the surface meaning is just the opposite, the image used by the Old Man suggests that judgment, not grace, hovers over Faustus's head. Only a few lines later he refers to Faustus's "hoplesse soule" (1299), and when Faustus goes off with Helen, the Old man calls him "Accursed Faustus" (1348).

The chorus closes *Doctor Faustus* with an allusion to Psalm 80.

> Cut is the branch that might have growne ful straight,
> And burned is Apollos Laurel bough,
> That sometime grew within this learned man.

"And the vineyard which thy right hand hathe planted, and the branch that thou madest strong for thyselfe; it is burned with fire, it is cut downe: they perish at the rebuke of thy countenance. . . . Turn us again, O Lord of hosts, cause thy face to shine; and we shalbe saved" (Ps. 80:15-16a, 19). The devils take Faustus away, but it is the rebuke of the countenance of God ("My God! My God! look not so fierce on me!" cries Faustus) that seals his doom. The branch that was strengthened for the service of God and might have grown full straight is cut and burned; Faustus is gone; his

---

through despair, has failed and willfully excluded the grace of heaven from his soul (1349; cf. Heb. 10:26-27). "My hearts so hardned I cannot repent" (629).

"waxen wings" have mounted "above his reach" (21) as "melting heavens conspirde his overthrow" (22). That God could have turned Faustus to himself whereas Faustus was powerless to repent was the view to which Faustus kept returning, and it was this fatalism, this casting of the full responsibility for salvation upon God instead of exercising faith, which makes the play a tragedy. If Faustus really had no choice of his own, there is no tragedy. Although the chorus closes the play with an allusion to a Scriptural passage which seems to support the view that Faustus held, Marlowe uses it as a basis for exhorting the wise to "Regard his hellish fall"— perhaps to emphasize that "the human will is always the observable agent of destruction and pain."[17] Both Barabas and John Faustus, particularly Faustus, owe much of their complexity and power as dramatic characters as well as much of the success of the plays in which they appear to the Marlovian looking-glass method of viewing Scripture, through which a reversal of conventional conceptions is accomplished and an additional force given to the dramatic statements.[18]

17. Cole, p. 260.
18. As indicated in earlier notes, that Marlowe also carefully included recognizable references to commonplaces of Renaissance theology and iconography is demonstrated by Hunter.

3. SHAKESPEARE: COMEDIES

Antonio, in *The Merchant of Venice*, says "The devil can cite Scripture for his purpose."[1] And Shakespeare, like Marlowe and other early English dramatists, gained certain dramatic effects by the citation of Scripture. Although his comedies show little or no Marlovian influence, at times ironic revelations of character appear, similar to those found in other dramatists. Serious Marlovian dramatic reversals of Scripture he reserved for the tragedies, though he used some humorous reversals with a serious point in the history plays.

The effects Shakespeare gains in his comedies may be broadly categorized. Misuses and misunderstandings of Scripture by comic characters result in enjoyment of the ludicrous. Certain familiar Biblical expressions used in popular Elizabethan jokes and proverbs add to the audience's delight in the fun. Sometimes Biblical allusion provides insight into particular characters, revealing an additional dimension and leading to a serious appraisal of human nature and behavior. And finally the Biblical echoes make the audience conscious of the moral and spiritual order of the universe in which the action takes place. The following representative examples in each of these categories by no means exhaust the possibilities. For example, in the section devoted to characterization, I have omitted fascinating characters like Portia and Shylock,[2] Feste and Sir Toby, and others, in order to concentrate on three who, taken together, suggest both the range and preciseness of Shakespeare's dramatic use of the Bible.

1. See Strathmann, "The Devil Can Cite Scripture," *Shakespeare 400*, pp. 17 ff. Surprisingly enough, this article includes no instance of the citation of Scripture in Shakespeare's works; the examples are merely illustrative of the playwright's revelation of man's hypocrisies in speech, both positive and negative.

2. See Nathan, "Balthasar, Daniel, and Portia"; Lewalski, "Biblical Allusion and Allegory in *The Merchant of Venice*." Lewalski presents such overwhelming evidence of the truth of her thesis—that "patterns of Biblical allusion and imagery are so precise and pervasive as to be patently deliberate . . . moreover . . . such language clearly reveals an important theological dimension in the play and points toward consistent and unmistakable allegorical meanings" (p. 328)—that it is not surprising that Roland Frye's condemnation of "theologizing analyses" does not mention it, not even in the bibliography (*Shakespeare and Christian Doctrine*).

Shakespeare's practice, throughout his career, of making comic characters twist Biblical words and phrases and shift Biblical concepts for a laugh is consonant with his love for word-play, punning, and witty repartee. In *The Comedy of Errors*, when Antipholus of Syracuse, suspicious of Ephesus and Ephesians anyway because of the talk he has heard about their practicing magic (a suspicion reminding one of the view of Ephesus given in Acts 19, where Ephesian converts made a bonfire of their books on sorcery),[3] is confronted by a courtesan friend of Antipholus of Ephesus, this dialogue takes place:

Ant. S. Satan, avoid! I charge thee, tempt me not!
Dro. S. Master, is this Mistress Satan?
Ant. S. It is the devil.
Dro. S. Nay, she is worse, she is the devil's dam,
    and here she comes in the habit of a light wench;
    and thereof comes that the wenches say, "God damn
    me"; that's as much as to say, God make me a light
    wench. It is written, they appear to men like
    angels of light; light is an effect of fire, and
    fire will burn; *ergo*, light wenches will burn. Come
    not near her. (IV.iii.48-58)

Antipholus, quite serious, uses Scriptural phrasing reminiscent of "Goe after me, Satan" (Matt. 16:23) to overcome temptation. Dromio, on the other hand, uses a Scriptural formula ("It is written") and quotation to make an off-color joke about venereal disease[4] by way of a ludicrous syllogism whose first premise is "Satan himselfe is transfourmed into an angel of light" (II Cor. 11:14).[5]

3. See Talbert, *Elizabethan Drama and Shakespeare's Early Plays*, p. 143, p. 365n30, for a concise and convincing analysis of how Shakespeare skillfully utilizes the commonplace thought of Ephesus as a town full of sorcerers and witches.

4. Dromio's joke may allude to Paul's use of "burn" in "it is better to marrie than to burne" (I Cor. 7:9). Shakespeare's audience heard frequently the eleventh homily "Against Whoredom and Adultery and Uncleanness" read from *Certain Sermons* with its final ringing admonition to the single to remember St. Paul's words. The "Come not near her," however, suggests some danger from wenches who "burn" those who come in contact with them. The OED cites this very usage in *The Comedy of Errors* as an example of the transitive verb meaning "to infect with sores; esp. with venereal disease."

5. This is perhaps the most frequently alluded to of all Scriptural passages used in Elizabethan drama. Another example of the deliberate twist of "light" is Falstaff's defense against the Chief Justice's charge that he follows the prince about like his ill angel: "Not so, my lord. Your ill angel is light; but I hope he that looks upon me will take me without weighing"(*II Henry IV*, I.ii.188-89).

Faustus who has sold his soul to the devil is made even more terrifying when that one has so reversed his moral and spiritual values that he applies to himself condemnatory Biblical passages which substitute the belly for God, shame for glory, and despair for faith.

A third use made by Marlowe of Biblical allusion reverses not only a value but the whole meaning of the original passage. An example is Barabas's curse on Abigail when he discovers that she has turned sincerely to Christianity and the life of a nun.

> Ne're shall she live to inherit ought of mine,
> Be blest of me, nor come within my gates,
> But perish underneath my bitter curse,
> Like *Cain* by *Adam,* for his brother's death.   (1332-35)

But the account of how Cain was actually cursed and by whom is quite different.[11] "Then the Lord said unto Kain . . . And now therefore thou art cursed from the earth, which hathe opened her mouth to receive thy brothers blood from thine hand. And the Lord set a marke upon Kain lest anie man finding him shoulde kil him" (Gen. 4:9a,11,15b). Adam did not curse his son; and the Lord, who did, also made provision for the protection of Cain so that he would not perish by violent means. Thus Barabas, by perverting a story of God's mercy even in judgment to a story of a father's vengeful curse, shows the way by which he can later feel justified in having murdered Abigail and the other nuns.

A fitting Scriptural epitaph for Barabas after all his machinations are over would be a text Marlowe does not use: "He that diggeth a pit, shal fall therein; and he that rolleth a stone, it shall returne upon him" (Prov. 26:27).[12]

In *Doctor Faustus* the opening scene in Faustus's study, containing the final rejection of divinity in favor of magic, turns on a reversal of meaning in the passages Faustus reads from Jerome's Latin Vulgate. The reversal is brought about, not by a perversion of the portion alluded to, but by a deletion of part of the context which considerably modifies the meaning of the portion read.

11. Cole, *Suffering and Evil in the Plays of Christopher Marlowe,* p. 127, notes this distortion of the Bible by Barabas but makes no point of it, failing to see in such distortion a consistent pattern.

12. Barabas's fall into a cauldron is shown by Hunter to have been reminiscent to Elizabethans of both Scripture (Job 41:11, 22) and familiar iconography of the period showing the covetous being punished in a boiling cauldron and Antichrist meeting the same doom (pp. 234-36).

Delilah's complexion, which, Moth assures Armado, was green. When Armado says, "My love is most immaculate white and red" (95-96), he is echoing a commonplace not necessarily Biblical, but he is also making an almost exact quotation of the Song of Solomon: "My love . . . is white and red" (Song 5:10). These references to Samson and Solomon are brought together a few lines later when Armado convinces himself that love has mastered him and justifies himself on the authority of these two Biblical worthies: "Yet was Samson so tempted, and he had an excellent strength; yet was Solomon so seduced, and he had a very good wit" (I.ii.178-81). The braggart identifies himself with Samson, though he will not even fight the swain Costard, and with Solomon, though he is so dense that even Moth can call him an ass to his face without his realizing it. That Armado so identifies himself is as ludicrous as Moth's joke about Samson with which his identification began.[7]

In *The Merry Wives of Windsor* Pistol often echoes Biblical phrases, as when he reports to Master Ford on Falstaff's affection for Mrs. Ford.

Ford. Why, sir, my wife is not young.
Pist. He woos both high and low, both rich and poor,
    Both young and old, one with another, Ford. (II.i.116-18)

This is very close to "As wel lowe as high, riche and poore, one with another" of Psalm 49:2. But the words of the psalm, which are familiar in a context of praise to God and of God's wisdom being dispersed to all the inhabitants of the earth, are now put in the bawdy context of Falstaff's undiscriminating desire to satisfy his "liver burning hot." But the best laugh in the play resulting from Biblical allusion comes when Pistol uses an expression repeated throughout Scripture (Ps. 44:1, Ezek. 24:26, etc.) and Parson Evans fails to recognize the phrase as Scriptural.

Fal. Pistol!
Pist. He hears with ears.
Evans. The tevil and his dam! What phrase is this, "He hears
    with ear"? Why, it is affectations.   (I.i.149-52)

7. Since Moth constantly shows contempt for, and makes wisecracks about, his master which Armado does not notice, it is very possible, as Thomas Pyles has suggested in a letter to me, that the name of Don Armado's page is itself a pun on the mote in the eye, as well as suggesting the insect. The pronunciation would have been the same as for "mote" [mo : t], and it is certain that, although Don Armado sees beams all around, he regards not the gibes of his own Moth.

If this incident is remembered, Shallow's later question of Sir Hugh Evans is particularly funny. Shallow asks, "What the sword and the word! Do you study them both, Master Parson?" (III.i.44-45). The obvious fear and nervousness of Evans which lead him to sing muddled fragments of Marlowe's "The Passionate Shepherd to his Love" together with a line from Psalm 37—"When as I sat in Pabylon"—and his failure to recognize Pistol's Biblical phrase make it sufficiently clear that Evans studies neither the sword nor the Word. Evans's inability to apply pastoral psychology is revealed by his simple-minded expostulation to a man who is in mortal fear of having been cuckolded: "Master Ford, you must pray, and not follow the imaginations of your own heart." Then he adds the enlightening comment, "This is jealousies" (IV.ii.162-63).

A variation on the theme of the proud Pharisee occurs in *The Winter's Tale* in Autolycus's conversation with the old shepherd and his son:

> How bless'd are we that are not simple men!
> Yet Nature might have made me as these are,
> Therefore I will not disdain.   (IV.iv.771-73)

In Christ's parable, "The Pharisee stood and prayed thus with himselfe, God, I thank thee, that I am not as other men are, extortioners, unjust, adulterers, or even as this publican" (Luke 18:11). The ludicrous element which gives rise to ironic humor is Autolycus's confident assurance that he is blessed so far above the shepherds, a great part of whose lives have been devoted to shielding Perdita, while Autolycus's life has been devoted to roguery and thievery. Still he is not quite like the Pharisee; his realization that he might have been made differently keeps him from the disdainful attitude of the man in the parable.

A similar use of allusion courts laughter by the use of Biblical expressions used jokingly by the Elizabethans. Here the laugh depends not so much on what the characters do to Scripture as on humorous associations with the Biblical phrase.

Perhaps partly because of the humorous presentation of the story in the early mystery plays and in such fabliaux as Chaucer's *Miller's Tale*, any reference to Noah and the flood would be good for a laugh. Shakespeare combines allusion to the past destruction of the earth by water with allusion to the future destruction of the earth by fire in *The Comedy of Errors*. Dromio and Antipholus of Syracuse discuss Luce, Adriana's servant:

33

over to Lucifer. At one point Faustus consoles himself with the thought: "Tush, Christ did call the thiefe upon the Crosse,/ Then rest thee Faustus quiet in conceit" (1147-48). But still the meaning of the Bible is reversed. His allusion is to the story of the repentant thief in the Gospel of Luke who said to Jesus, "Lord, remember me when thou comest into thy kingdome" (Luke 23:42). It is not Christ who calls the thief (Marlowe may have intended Faustus's use of "call" in the theological sense of the supernatural drawing by the Spirit of the elect, as in the phrase "calling and election," used by Calvinists), but it is the thief who calls upon Christ, believing that Christ will receive him. Faustus wavers in fear and thinks of Christ and his saving blood, but instead of calling to Christ as the thief did, he calls upon Lucifer to spare him and upon the mountains and hills to fall upon him and hide him. After seeing the blood of Christ momentarily, he says:

> Where is it now? 'tis gone: And see where God
> Stretcheth out his arme, and bends his irefull browes:
> Mountaines and hilles, come, come, and fall on me,
> And hide me from the heavy wrath of God.   (1436-39)

Here, in the moment of his end, Faustus's allusion to the Bible emphasizes his despair:[15] according to Scripture, when God's judgment upon earth was envisioned in the Apocalypse, the great men of the nations hid themselves "and said to the mountaines and rockes, fall on us, and hide us from the presence of him that sitteth on the throne, & from the wrath of the Lambe" (Rev. 6:16).

The function of the Old Man in Scene xiii seems to be in the early English tradition of having a reliable commentator on the events in the play—one who, like the Doctor in the mystery cycles, can be counted on to give the audience the "right" view. Almost everything the Old Man says to Faustus is traceable to Bible texts,[16]

15. In seeing Faustus as damned for lack of faith, i.e., despair, rather than for the sin of demoniality, I am agreeing with Davidson, "Doctor Faustus of Wittenberg," rather than with Greg, "The Damnation of Faustus." Davidson's view, as his citations to Melanchthon help demonstrate, is in accord with Reformation theology, as is Campbell's. Greg cites a seventeenth century Catholic theologian, the Rev. Lodovico Sinistrari.

16. Significant speeches of the Old Man are: Lines 1283-84 (Rev. 1:5), 1291-94 (Rev. 16:1), and 1351-56 (Luke 22:31-32, I Pet. 1:7, Ps. 2:4). The Old Man is a foil to Faustus; when "Sathan begins to sift" the Old Man (1351), he stands the test as Peter did (Luke 22:31-32), and Mephistophilis says, "His faith is great, I cannot touch his soule" (1316; cf. Matt. 10:28); but Faustus,

raises a question (or perhaps answers one) about Jaquenetta.[9] Another familiar expression used by Don Armado of Jaquenetta in his letter to the king concerning his apprehension of the lawbreaking lovers indicates that she and Costard were engaged in a more than casual relationship. "For Jaquenetta—so is the weaker vessel called which I apprehended with the aforesaid swain—I keep her as a vessel of thy law's fury" (I.i.275-78). The expression "weaker vessel" appears in Scripture (I Pet. 3:7) where it clearly means a wife; the term was widely used during the Elizabethan period to mean any woman, but with sexual connotation.[10]

Another such Biblical phrase, usually connected with marriage by Shakespeare's audience, is "to go to the world." The clown in *All's Well That Ends Well* says to the Countess Rousillon: "No, madam, 'tis not so well that I am poor, though many of the rich are damn'd; but, if I may have your ladyship's good will to go to the world, Isbel the woman and I will do as we may" (I.iii.17-21). His reference to the damning of the rich recalls the simile of the camel and the needle's eye (Mark 10:25) and the story of Dives and Lazarus (Luke 16), but the special point of consideration here is his use of the phrase "to go to the world," meaning to marry. This expression may have arisen from the complaint of Lot's daughter just before she and her sister made their father drunk and lay with him; though Sodom and Gomorrah were destroyed, their spirit lived on in the daughters. The complaint of the eldest was, "there is not a man to come in unto us after the manner of all the worlde" (Gen. 19:32). Two other possible sources are Paul's statement that "she that is married, careth for the things that pertaine to the worlde, howe she may please her husband"(I Cor. 7:34) and Jesus's observation, "The children of this worlde marrie wives, and are married" (Luke 20:34). Whether one or all of these texts is the

9. That the expression is not always suggestive of sex, however, is shown by Hal's reference to Bardolph's red nose: "O villain, thou stolest a cup of sack eighteen years ago, and wert taken with the manner, and ever since thou hast blush'd extempore" (*I Henry IV*, II.iv.345-47). As a proverb Tilley traces the phrase back to 1530; however, the first clear use of it in the Biblical sense is Costard's, next Hal's, then a use in 1606. Tilley does not identify the Bible as the source. On similar puns by Costard see Talbert, *Elizabethan Drama*, pp. 238-40.

10. In *Romeo and Juliet*, Sampson shows that a reference to "weak" could as soon bring up "vessel" as vice versa and a joke be made of the combination. To Gregory's comment that "the weakest goes to the wall" Sampson retorts, " 'Tis true; and therefore women, being the weaker vessels, are ever thrust to the wall" (I.i.19-22).

source of the popular phrase, the main point made here is that it is Biblical and that it has the effect of producing laughter in an audience familiar with it as part of the common idiom.

After having referred to marriage as "to go to the world," the clown in *All's Well That Ends Well* proceeds to use slightly twisted Biblical allusions to justify his desire to marry. He gives three reasons: he desires the blessing of God and "barnes are blessings" (I.iii.28), alluding to "children are an heritage of the Lord, and the fruit of the wombe is his reward" (Ps. 127:4); his body is "driven on by the flesh" (32) toward marriage, alluding to "it is better to marrie than to burne" (I Cor. 7:9); and he wishes to marry that he may repent and be saved (39), alluding to the promise that "the unbelieving husband is sanctified by the wife" (I Cor. 7:14). This clown, "shrewd and unhappy" as Lafeu calls him, a veritable fountain of Scripture, will be considered again later.

Audrey, in *As You Like It*, uses the popular and Biblical expression for marriage in discussing her own forthcoming union with Touchstone when she says, "I do desire it with all my heart; and I hope it is no dishonest desire to desire to be a woman of the world" (V.iii.3-5). Nowhere, perhaps, is her naïveté, of which Touchstone seeks to take advantage, shown clearer than in this allusion with its slight suggestion of bawdiness.

But it remained for Beatrice of *Much Ado About Nothing* to use the expression to good humorous effect and to couple it with another popular joke based on Scripture; Beatrice puts both in one breath. "Good Lord, for alliance! Thus goes every one to the world but I, and I am sunburnt. I may sit in a corner and cry 'Heigh-ho for a husband!'" (II.i.330-32). Prior to the prayer book revision of 1662, the Biblical promise "The sun shall not burn thee by day: neither the moon by night" (Ps. 121:6) was read on the occasion of the service called the "Churching of Women," a service for women who had recently borne children. The Scriptural verse came to be a standard joke about married women being, literally, overshadowed by their husbands. Beatrice is saying, while everyone else goes the way of the world and gets married, thereby being shaded from the sun by a husband, I am free and the sun burns me. That another psalm was substituted for Psalm 121 when the prayer book was revised in 1662 indicates that the joke was current and the use of the psalm indecorous.[11]

11. Noble, pp. 29-30.

Supporting the interpretation of "sunburnt" is another Biblical allusion which Beatrice uses earlier in the scene just quoted.

> *Leon.* Well, niece, I hope to see you one day fitted
> with a husband.
> *Beat.* Not till God make men of some other metal than
> earth. Would it not grieve a woman to be over-
> master'd with a piece of valiant dust? To make
> an account of her life to a clod of wayward marl?
> No, uncle, I'll none. Adam's sons are my brethren;
> and truly, I hold it a sin to match my kindred.
>
> (II.i.60-67)

Through the witty turn she gives to the Biblical statement that man was formed "from the dust of the earth" (Gen. 2:7) she asks: Why should woman, whose origin from a rib of man is higher than man's origin from clay, be subjected to man? Furthermore, she caps her rejoinder with a demonstration that none can marry without committing incest. What can be done with such dazzling female logic, which proves the superiority of the female and the sinfulness of marriage by arguing from a Biblical premise to a *reductio ad absurdum?*

The use of Biblical allusion to add another dimension to particular characters is the most prominent of the ways Shakespeare uses the Bible in his comedies. From the quantity of material available, I have chosen to limit this discussion to three characters taken from the comedies: Biron from the early period (*Love's Labour's Lost*), Angelo from the middle period (*Measure for Measure*), and Prospero from the late period (*The Tempest*).

From the beginning of *Love's Labour's Lost* Biron is recognized as the most sensible one of the king's circle. Although he is willing to subscribe to a three-year period of study, he balks at going without sleep, at fasting, and especially at giving up feminine companionship. He has a conviction about oaths. When the king insists that Biron has sworn to abide by all the restrictions, Biron replies, "By yea and nay, sir, then I swore in jest" (I.i.54). His "yea and nay" recall Jesus's injunction "sweare not at al . . . but let your communication be, Yea, yea; Nay, nay; for whatsoever is more than these commeth of evil" (Matt. 5:34a, 37a).[12] Biron suggests, further,

---

12. In the sermon "Against Swearing and Perjury," the patristic authority of Jerome, Chrysostom, and Theophylactus was added to the words of Jesus. *Certain Sermons*, p. 46.

that the king will have to break the article forbidding talk with a woman, since the Princess of France is coming on an official visit. The king admits that "mere necessity" will cause him to break this one article. Says Biron:

> Necessity will make us all forsworn
> Three thousand times within this three years' space;
> For every man with his affects is born,
> Not by might mast'red, but by special grace.   (I.i.150-53)

The concept of man's need of divine grace to overcome the sinful inclinations of his nature appears repeatedly in the Bible, as in Paul's "Let us have grace, whereby we may serve God acceptably" (Heb. 12:28).

Such Biblical allusions invite the audience to consider Biron as more than a "merry mad-cap lord" whose every word is in jest; he is also an intelligent man with insight into human nature and its weaknesses. Even when Biron realizes that he has fallen in love with Rosaline, he recognizes human nature's inclination to succumb to temptation; though he expresses amazement at his love, his fall is more excusable than the loves of the other lords, who have been so self-assured. Biron expostulates:

> What! I love! I sue! I seek a wife!
> A woman that is like a German clock,
> Still a-repairing, ever out of frame,
> And never going aright, being a watch,
> But being watch'd that it may still go right!
>
> . . . .
>
> And I to sigh for her! to watch for her!
> To pray for her!   (III.i.191-95, 202-3)

The proximity of "watch" and "pray" when taken with the meaning of the passage (that Biron has been attracted against his will) reminds one of Jesus's "Watch and pray, lest ye enter into temptation" (Matt. 26:41).

Though he watches and prays, it is for the wrong divinity. Then, hidden from sight, he learns of the loves of the king and Longaville and says, "God amend us, God amend! We are much out o' th' way" (IV.iii.76), with reference to the apostle's description of man's depravity, "They are all gone out of the waye . . . there is none that doeth good, no, not one" (Rom. 3:12). Then Dumain, reading his love poem, is challenged by Longaville, Longaville by the king, and Biron steps forth to "whip hypocrisy" in others.

> But are you not asham'd? Nay, are you not,
> All three of you to be thus o'er shot?
> You found his mote; the King your mote did see;
> But I a beam do find in each of three.   (IV.iii.159-62)

Of course, the audience knows that Biron's makes the fourth beam;
he who would whip hypocrisy is playing the hypocrite himself in
his reference to the Bible: "Thou hypocrite, cast out the beame out
of thine own eye first, & then shall thou see perfectly to put out the
moate that is in thy brothers eye" (Luke 6:42).

When Biron's own beam is discovered, he begins to defend Rosaline's beauty in Scriptural terms. Of her brunette features, he says,
"O, 'tis the sun that maketh all things shine. . . . No face is fair that
is not full so black" (IV.iii.246, 253), alluding to the bride's description of herself in Solomon's song of songs: "I am black, but comely.
. . . I am black, because the sun hath looked upon me" (Song
1:5-6).

Chosen by the others to prove their loving lawful, Biron caps a
long passage of eloquent defense of love with two Biblical allusions.

> Let us once lose our oaths to find ourselves,
> Or else we lose ourselves to keep our oaths.
> It is religion to be thus forsworn,
> For charity itself fulfills the law,
> And who can sever love from charity?   (IV.iii.361-65)

The first two lines are a variation of "whosoever will save his life
shal loose it: againe, who so ever will loose his life for my sake shal
finde it" (Matt. 16:25), and the crowning argument for oath-break-
ing as a religious act is "the fulfilling of the lawe is charitie" (Rom.
13:10). As the wittiest and most articulate of the group, Biron is
the appropriate one to state the lovers' apologia; even more important, however, he has recognized, on Scriptural grounds, the futility
of such oaths as they have made without divine grace to help them
overcome their natural desires.[13] Biron is enriched in intellect, in-
tegrity, and sincerity by his use of Biblical allusion.

13. Sermon VII, "Against Swearing and Perjury," *Certain Sermons*, p. 45,
probably remembered if only subliminally by the audience, lends authority to
Biron's words: "But if a man at any time, either of ignorance, or of malice,
promise and swear to do any thing which is either against the law of Almighty
God, or not in his power to perform: let him take it for an unlawful and ungodly oath." In such circumstances, the homily makes clear to the "good Christian people," the devout are constrained by their devotion to break the ungodly
oath.

Measure for Measure, the title of which is from the text "With what measure ye mete, it shalbe measured to you againe" (Matt. 7:2b), is what Bonamy Dobrée calls "great comedy," as distinguished from "free" and "critical comedy," because of its concern with the great issues of life (such as hypocrisy, the exercise of power) and because it borders on tragedy.[14] The character of Angelo gives the play this particular kind of greatness, for the main action depends on his assumption of power and his peculiar brand of cloistered virtue. One of the chief ways Shakespeare gives us insight into the character of Angelo (and, by extension, into truth about human nature in general) is the use of Biblical allusion, both in the speeches of Angelo himself and in the references to him by other characters.[15]

The Duke provides the first hints as to the kind of virtue Angelo has and how we may expect it to stand the test of full authority in Vienna. The Duke says to Angelo:

> Heaven doth with us as we with torches do,
> Not light them for themselves; for if our virtues
> Did not go forth of us, 'twere all alike
> As if we had them not.　　　　　　　　　　　　(I.i.33-36)

The allusion is to a familiar saying: "Neyther doe menne light a candel, and put it under a busshel, but on a candelsticke; and it giveth light unto al that are in the house. Let your light so shine before menne, that they may see your good workes, and gloryfie your father, whiche is in heaven" (Matt. 5:15-16).

It is the Duke's purpose to remove the bushel that Angelo's light may shine, to allow his virtue to "sally forth," in order to see how this light, this virtue, will react to responsibilities. Another hint of forthcoming developments is provided by the Duke when he says, "We have with a leaven'd and prepared choice/ Proceeded to you; therefore take your honours" (I.i.52-53), recalling Jesus's admonition: "Beware of the leven of the Pharisees, whiche is hypocrisie" (Luke 12:1). The suggestion here that the Duke's purpose is to try Angelo for suspected hypocrisy is soon confirmed by the Duke's words to Friar Thomas.

14. *Restoration Comedy*, pp. 15-16.

15. The hypothesis has been advanced that the delineation of Angelo's character was "an experiment by Shakespeare: an attempt to handle, in a comedy, a character comparable to the characters of the tragedies." Dodds, "The Character of Angelo in 'Measure for Measure,'" p. 255. See also Pope, "The Renaissance Background of *Measure for Measure*."

40

> Lord Angelo is precise,
> Stands at a guard with envy, scarce confesses
> That his blood flows, or that his appetite
> Is more to bread than stone; hence shall we see
> If power change purpose, what our seemers be.
>
> (I.iii.50-54)

In other words, Angelo is so proud of his virtue that he even sets himself above Christ, who when tempted did not deny that his appetite was to bread rather than stone, but, instead, insisted that bread is not enough (Matt. 4:3-4).

The Duke's test reveals Angelo to the world as a fallible man, but it also reveals Angelo to himself. He of whom the Duke said that he would scarce confess that his blood flowed and of whom Lucio said, "his blood/ Is very snow-broth" (I.iv.58), has to come face to face with his own nature and confess, "Blood, thou art blood" (II.iv.15). He recognizes his own hypocrisy:

> Heaven in my mouth,
> As if I did but only chew his name,
> And in my heart the strong and swelling evil
> Of my conception. (II.iv.4-7)

The allusion is clear: "This people draweth nigh unto me with their mouth, and honoureth me with their lippes; howbeit their hart is farre from me" (Quoted from Isa. in Matt. 15:8). (Angelo's reference to "his name" indicates that the "Heaven" of his speech was originally "God"; the name of the deity was often omitted when a play was printed.) Isabella, later in the same scene, exclaims,

> O perilous mouths,
> That bear in them one and the self-same tongue,
> Either of condemnation or approof. (II.iv.172-74)

Isabella echoes James 3:10: "Out of one mouth proceedeth blessing and cursing." Thus Angelo is an unforgettable example of the Biblical doctrine that virtue is not true virtue unless it can stand the test of temptation; and the most severe temptation of all comes when one has the power of life and death over other human beings.[16]

16. I have avoided pushing Biblical parallels to the typological extreme that others have felt the play justifies. See Battenhouse, *"Measure for Measure and the Christian Doctrine of Atonement."* Battenhouse's extreme view invites the sarcasm of Roland Frye's comment that Battenhouse makes of Mariana "perhaps the most droll of the Christ-analogues" (*Shakespeare*, p. 36).

In *The Tempest* Prospero's character as almost a divinity of the island is heightened by Biblical allusions which associate him with Christ as well as portray him as a sort of benevolent deity who has cast his pearls before swine in seeking to educate the savage Caliban.

Prospero refers to those in the tempest-tossed ship:

> No, not so much perdition as an hair
> Betid to any creature in the vessel
> Which thou heard'st cry, which thou saw'st sink.
>
> (I.ii.30-32)

This is much like Paul's assurance to those involved in the shipwreck of Acts: "There shal not an hair fal from the head of any of you" (Acts 27:34). But Ariel's[17] report to Prospero later evokes the "fourth man like to the Sonne of God" who protected the three Hebrews in the fiery furnace, "upon whome the fire had no manner of power in their bodies: insomuche that the very hair of their head was not burnt and their clothes unchanged, yea there was no smell of fire felt upon them" (Dan. 3:27). Ariel describes the survivors thus:

> Not a hair perish'd;
> On their sustaining garments not a blemish,
> But fresher than before.   (I.ii.217-19)

When Caliban says to Prospero, "Thou . . . wouldst . . . teach me how/ To name the bigger light, and how the less,/ That burn by day and night" (I.ii.334-36), one glimpses a vision of Prospero patiently seeking to teach the monster Caliban the great Bible stories, such as that of creation, when "God made two great lightes; a greater light to rule the day, and the lesser light to rule the night" (Gen. 1:16). But the extent of Prospero's failure to Christianize Caliban is measured not only by Caliban's attempt to ravish Miranda but also by his use of Biblical allusion when he says to Stephano, speaking of Prospero, "I'll yield him thee asleep,/ Where thou mayst

17. That Ariel is probably a variant of Uriel, "the light of God," is pointed out by Macht, "Biblical Allusion in Shakespeare's 'The Tempest' in the Light of Hebrew Exegesis" (cf. Noble, p. 251). Macht sees parallels between Jonah 1:5-6 and *The Tempest*, I.i.54, and between Job 14:10 and IV.i.156-58. He connects Prospero's epithet for Caliban, "Thou earth!" (I.ii.314) with the Hebrew *adamah*. The contention of Macht that Shakespeare knew the Hebrew Bible is hardly tenable on the evidence presented. The examples cited could have been drawn from the marginal notes in the English Bible.

knock a nail into his head" (III.ii.68-69). Such stories of cruelty as Jael's killing Sisera (Judg. 4:21) are all that Caliban retains of the Bible.[18]

In the last act, Prospero's allusions associate him with both the humanity and the divinity of Christ. He says to Ariel concerning those who were shipwrecked:

> Hast thou, which art but air, a touch, a feeling
> Of their afflictions, and shall not myself,
> One of their kind, that relish all as sharply
> Passion as they, be kindlier mov'd than thou art?
>
> (V.i.21-24)

Prospero's words recall Christ as the High Priest: "For we have not an hie priest whiche cannot be touched with the feeling of our infirmities; but was in all pointes tempted like as we are, yet without sinne" (Heb. 4:15). The identification is given more force when it is remembered that an earlier chapter of the Epistle to the Hebrews seeks to show how Christ is an especially fitting high priest for man, since he is not a spiritual being like an angel, or like Ariel, but is a man "made like unto his brethren that he mighte be mercifull." Thus Prospero's forgiveness is Christ-like. Prospero even claims Christ-like power:

> graves at my command
> Have wak'd their sleepers, op'd, and let 'em forth
> By my so potent art.   (V.i.48-50)

Only after the action of the play is over is Prospero, in the Epilogue, a man of human strength only. To the last of the play he is a divinity who can promise "calm seas, auspicious gales" like Christ, who calmed the waves and stilled the winds (Mark 4:39). Such allusions keep Prospero out of the realm of Faustian black magic, in spite of references to his "books" and "rough magic," and maintain the audiences sympathy towards him.

Shakespeare sometimes uses Biblical allusion to make the audi-

18. An allusion to the Jael-Sisera story in the reign of Mary might have gotten quite a different response. John Ponet, author of the Edwardian catechism, in *A Short Treatise of politike power, and of the true Obedience which Subjects owe to kyngs and other Civile Governours* (1556), had cited Jael along with other Biblical characters as a justification of tyrannicide. See Talbert, *The Problem of Order*, pp. 73-74. Under Elizabeth and James, the Jael story might seem seditious (if Ponet's use was recalled); thus it is an appropriate story for the rebellious Caliban to allude to.

ence conscious of the setting of the local, limited action within the broader setting of a moral and spiritual universe. Such a consciousness, involved implicitly in some of the material already discussed, is especially noteworthy in *All's Well That Ends Well.* In spite of the immorality and boorishness of Bertram and the substitution of Helena for Diana as the subject of Bertram's amour, the action of the play is set squarely within a moral universe where Good and Evil, God and the Devil, and Heaven and Hell are real. The universal setting is suggested by the clown's allusion-packed speech, a speech carefully tagged (by words put in the mouth of Lafeu) to be taken seriously by the audience. The clown has mentioned serving a prince.

> *Lafeu.* What prince is that?
> *Clown.* The Black Prince, sir; alias, the prince of darkness; alias the devil.
> *Lafeu.* Hold thee, there's my purse. I give thee not this to suggest thee from thy master thou talk'st of. Serve him still.
> *Clown.* I am a woodland fellow, sir, that always loved a great fire; and the master I speak of ever keeps a good fire. But, sure, he is the prince of the world; let his nobility remain in's court. I am for the house with the narrow gate, which I take to be too little for pomp to enter. Some that humble themselves may; but the many will be too chill and tender, and they'll be for the flow'ry way that leads to the broad gate and the great fire.
> *Lafeu.* [After the clown's exit] A shrewd knave and an unhappy. (IV.v.44-58)

Many texts are alluded to in the clown's speech (among them Eph. 6:12, Matt. 25:41; John 14:2, John 16:11, Matt. 18:4) but particularly significant is the saying of Jesus, "Enter ye in at the straite gate; for wide is the gate and broad is the way that leadeth to destruction, and many there be whiche goe in thereat" (Matt. 7:13).[19] The clown's words are consistent with the theme of the play and give that theme broader implications: all that seems well is not unless it ends well; the "flow'ry way" is attractive except for its destination, which is the "great fire." On the other hand, the narrow

19. The Rheims version of this text, contrasting "narrow gate" and "brode gate," is closer to Shakespeare here than the Bishops' Bible.

44

way is arduous and requires humility in those who choose it, but it ends well. As the King puts it, for Diana, Helena, and Bertram:

> All yet seems well; and if it end so meet,
> The bitter past, more welcome is the sweet.
>
> (V.iii.333-34)

4. SHAKESPEARE: HISTORIES AND TRAGEDIES

In the history plays and the tragedies Shakespeare underscores theme and foreshadows action by Biblical allusion, a practice similar to that noted earlier in *Eastward Ho!* and he follows the Marlovian practice of reversal of Biblical allusions. Although he uses the Bible for humorous development of the ludicrous and the familiar in the histories and tragedies as well as in the comedies, a larger purpose is served. This chapter emphasizes allusion for characterization, both in what is said about a character and in what that character himself says. It illustrates a method of underscoring theme and anticipating future lines of development in the action. Finally, it examines dramatic reversals of Scripture, both of Marlowe's kind and of kinds peculiar to Shakespeare.

From the many possibilities in Shakespeare's histories and tragedies[1] I have chosen six characters from four plays to exemplify serious character delineation: two heroines (Juliet and Desdemona), two princes (Prince Hal and Hamlet), and two villains (Claudius and Iago).

When Romeo informs Friar Laurence that he is no longer interested in Rosaline and wishes to marry Juliet, the clergyman is amazed that the young man's love could shift so soon. Romeo explains that his newly found love reciprocates his affection: "I pray thee, chide me not. Her I love now/ Doth grace for grace and love for love allow" (II.iii.85-86). He uses a Biblical phrase about Christ: "And of his fulnesse have al we received, and grace for grace" (John 1:16). That Romeo should worship Juliet as more than mortal woman, as his language associating her with Christ indicates, is especially appropriate since one scene earlier she has called him "the god of my idolatry." When in that scene her lover begins to

---

1. For example, Biblical allusion in *Macbeth*, excluded from this study, has received a good deal of attention elsewhere. For a discussion of the possible influence of the Bible as interpreted in a sermon by King James, see Jack, "*Macbeth*, King James, and the Bible"; see also Frye, "Macbeth's Usurping Wife"; Siegel, "Echoes of the Bible Story in *Macbeth*"; Elliott, *Dramatic Providence in Macbeth*.

swear faithfulness by the moon, Juliet stops him for fear that if he swears by something so inconstant, his love will prove variable too.

Rom. What shall I swear by?
Jul.   Do not swear at all;
        Or, if thou wilt, swear by the gracious self,
        Which is the god of my idolatry,
        And I'll believe thee.   (II.ii.112-15)

The girl begins by urging him to observe Jesus's injunction to "Sweare not at al" (Matt. 5:34), but shifts suddenly to identify Romeo with God, who "because he coulde sweare by no greater, he sware by himselfe" (Heb. 6:13). Then, before he can say more than five words, she interrupts to say, "Well, do not swear" (II.ii. 117). These passages emphasize how extravagant is their love. At the same time, when Juliet changes from "Do not swear" to "swear by thy . . . self" to "do not swear" again,[2] the Biblical allusions help portray her character as both impulsive and hesitant, both firm of mind and vacillating; in short, she is a combination of paradoxical elements.

Other allusions confirm this paradoxical nature while they underscore the theme of the "star-cross'd lovers," for whom everything turns out badly just when appearances indicate that things will turn out well. Hearing the news of Tybalt's death from the nurse and assuming, from the nurse's garbled account, that Romeo is also dead, Juliet asks,

        Is Romeo slaught'red, and is Tybalt dead?
        My dearest cousin, and my dearest lord?
        Then, dreadful trumpet, sound the general doom!
        For who is living, if those two are gone?   (III.ii.65-68)

In hyperbole she alludes to the day of judgment, when "the trumpe shal blowe and the dead shal rise incorruptable, and we

2. Juliet's return to "do not swear" would recall to many minds the Elizabethan homily "Against Swearing and Perjury," where Christ's "swear not at all" (Matt. 5:34) was interpreted in the light of patristic authority. "For every Christian mans word (saith S. Hierome) should be so true, that it should be regarded as an oath. And Chrysostome witnessing the same, saith, It is not convenient to swear: for what needeth us to swear, when it is not lawful for one of us to lie to another? . . . For truth is (as Theophylactus writeth) that no man is less trusted than he that useth much to swear" (*Certain Sermons*, p. 46). Juliet's conclusion, then, may have gotten the same reaction from the audience as if she had said, "Well, a man who overswears is less to be trusted than one who lets his communication be simply yea and nay."

shalbe changed" (I Cor. 15:52b). But a few minutes later, when the nurse reveals that Romeo killed Tybalt, the impulsive mind of Juliet makes another of its swings. After calling Romeo a "wolvish ravening lamb," alluding to the Biblical warning about those who come "in sheepes clothing, but inwardly they are revening woolfes" (Matt. 7:15), she says,

> O nature, what hadst thou to do in hell,
> When thou didst bower the spirit of a fiend
> In mortal paradise of such sweet flesh?   (III.ii.80-82)

Still clinging to the idea of Romeo as her divinity, she remembers the warning that at times "Satan himselfe is transfourmed into an angel of light" (II Cor. 11:14), and wonders if this has happened in her lover.

The common element in all Juliet's Biblical allusions is paradox, a wavering between alternative attitudes. Such paradox is basic to the theme of the play with its contrast between the love of the young and the hate of the old, the best-laid plans of men and the vagaries of fateful circumstance. And at the heart of the play stands simple, naïve young maidenhood, undergoing a struggle between head and heart, always faithful, in spite of fears and doubts, to the man she loves, but thwarted by old circumstances of enmity from being fully united with him in life because of "misadventur'd piteous overthrows." Although both her inner struggles and the outer obstacles that thwart her and Romeo are well delineated aside from the Biblical allusions, these add to the effectiveness of the characterization.

Quite different in other ways, Desdemona does share the simplicity and innocence of mind of Juliet; she, too, has the courage to act independently in choosing the man she will marry, but, caught in Iago's web, she is defeated by her own frankness, innocence, and inexperience. The speeches of Othello contain most of the Biblical allusions characterizing Desdemona, but she herself is given at least one. When Othello first confronts her with his charge that she has been unfaithful, he asks, "Are not you a strumpet?" Desdemona answers,

> No, as I am a Christian.
> If to preserve this vessel for my lord
> From any other foul unlawful touch
> Be not to be a strumpet, I am none.   (IV.ii.82-85)

Desdemona's words recall, appropriately, a passage enjoining Christians to sexual purity: "ye should absteine from fornication . . . everyone of you shoulde knowe howe to possess his vessel in holiness and honour" (I Thess. 4:3b-4). Desdemona's Christian purity stands out sharply against the dark background of suspicion; she preserves her lord's vessel while he calls her whore and acts as though he were a paying customer. Desdemona's answer heightens appreciation for her chaste character.

Both the lowest condemnation of Desdemona and her highest praise come in Biblical language. Having smothered her, Othello at first pretends to Emilia that he is innocent. Desdemona revives enough to speak and claims to have killed herself.

> *Oth.* She's, like a liar, gone to burning hell.
>   'Twas I that kill'd her.
> *Emil.*   O, the more angel she,
>   And you the blacker devil!
> *Oth.* She turn'd to folly, and she was a whore.
> *Emil.* Thou dost belie her, and thou art a devil.
> *Oth.* She was false as water.   (V.ii.138-44)

Othello alludes to the statement that "all liers shal have their part in the lake which burneth with fire and brimstone" (Rev. 21:8b), and to Jacob's analysis of his son Reuben as "unstable as water" (Gen. 49:4a) because the son had committed adultery with a concubine of Jacob's. The effect is heavily ironic, for Othello thinks of himself as having in righteous indignation snuffed out a wicked woman, while Emilia and we know that he has, like a devil, taken the life of a saintly angel.[3]

---

3. I do not intend the reader to mistake Shakespeare's metaphors "devil" and "angel" here for reality. Bethell, "Shakespeare's Imagery: The Diabolic Images in *Othello*," and Siegel, "The Damnation of Othello," both see Othello damned to Hell and Desdemona translated to Heaven partly on the basis of these words. For a plea for more emphasis on the donnée in a play and less (or none) on the matters of "peripheral importance," see Hubler, "The Damnation of Othello: Some Limitations of the Christian View of the Play." Although the acceptance (see below) of the Folio reading "Judean" and its consequent association of Othello with Judas Iscariot leads one to think of Judas's suicide and death condemning him to Hell, one is not justified, in my opinion, in extrapolating a dramatic character's eternal destiny in any dogmatic fashion, even if the text seems to invite it. The existence of strong arguments from the same text for Othello's salvation (e.g., Ribner, *Patterns in Shakespearian Tragedy*) and for his damnation indicate that Shakespeare was appealing more to his audience's "ability to see the many-sidedness of things" (Hubler, p. 299) than to its orthodox theological convictions. As Hubler would have to admit, how-

Before being convinced of Desdemona's innocence, Othello has said of her:

> Had she been true,
> If Heaven would make me such another world
> Of one entire and perfect chrysolite,
> I'd not have sold her for it. (V.ii.143-46)

After Iago's diabolic plot has been revealed, too late, Othello again compares Desdemona to a precious stone, this time to a pearl, and he compares himself to "the base Judean" who "threw a pearl away/ Richer than all his tribe" (V.ii.347-48).[4] In Othello's speech, then, Desdemona, more precious than a world of chrysolite, becomes associated with the "pearl of great price" of the Bible, for which a merchant "went and sold all that he had, and bought it" (Matt. 13:46). But Othello, unlike the merchant, has thrown the pearl away like the "base Judean." The reference recalls Judas Iscariot, who by betraying Christ discarded the Messiah. The Folio reading "Judean" (rather than the Quarto's "Indian"), meaning Judas, is substantiated by Othello's words as he kills himself: "I kiss'd thee ere I kill'd thee: no way but this,/ Killing myself, to die upon a kiss. (V.ii.358-59). Judas betrayed his Master with a kiss and later killed himself. The character of Othello is thus associated

---

ever, one of those many sides is the possibility of Othello's winding up in the orthodox Hell which his own words seem to describe (V.ii.227-80), though Hubler suggests, in violation of his own thesis, that Othello could be describing purgatory. See also Barnet, "Some Limitations of a Christian Approach to Shakespeare": "The rigidly Christian interpretation forces a tragedy to fit ideas which Shakespeare doubtless held but did not dramatize" (p. 92).

4. Graham Greene, in *The Heart of the Matter* (New York, 1948), has Yusef the Syrian associate himself with "the base Indian . . . who threw a pearl away" because he lost the possibility of friendship with Major Scobie by betraying and blackmailing him. Since Yusef's betrayal of Scobie is the direct cause of Scobie's suicide (like Christ's death, his is voluntarily met for the love of others, but the treachery is instrumental), the Folio reading would have been much more effective as an allusion. This is noted here merely as an example of how much of the depth of Shakespeare's meaning continues to be lost by accepting the easier reading of the Quarto. The internal evidence of association between the pearl and Desdemona and the kiss that precedes the killing convinces me that the better reading is "Judean"; "Indian" must be accompanied by such a lame note as that in the Neilson and Hill edition: "The allusion has not been identified" (p. 1135, fn. to V.ii.347), or it must be given such weak support as that Shakespeare recalled earlier stories of Moors being careless with pearls and had Othello "with signal patriotism [change] the nationality of the ignorant culprit." Freeman, "Othello's 'Base Indian.'" This ignores Othello's signal lack of both pride and patriotism in likening himself to a "turbaned Turk."

with a Judas possessed by Satan (John 13:2), as Othello is mentally poisoned by Iago.[5]

Sympathy for Desdemona is increased by Biblical allusion, both as it is used in unjust disparagement of her and in just praise.

Although it is primarily in *Henry V* that Shakespeare elevates the dignity and seriousness of the hero-prince to the height necessary for the ideal king, promise of coming reform occurs as early as the first act of *I Henry IV* and is made more effective by Biblical language. In a soliloquy explaining why he keeps such company as he does, the Prince asserts that beauty or worth is more appreciated when it unexpectedly appears against a contrasting setting ("like bright metal on a sullen ground"). The soliloquy closes with this couplet: "I'll so offend, to make offence a skill,/ Redeeming time when men think least I will" (I.ii.239-40). The phrase is Paul's: "Walke in wisdome towarde them that are without, redeeming the time" (Col. 4:5) and "walke circumspectlie, not as fooles, but as wise, redeeming the time, because the days are evil" (Eph. 5:15-16). Thus the audience is assured that Hal's mature virtues will shine all the brighter against the background of his earlier days.

J. A. Bryant, Jr., discusses "Prince Hal and the Ephesians," but instead of dealing with the effect of the allusions noted here, moves on to point out other connections, tenuous though they be, to Paul's epistle to the Ephesians. However, Bryant does note in *II Henry IV* two echoes of Hal's "redeeming the time": "playing fool with the time" (II.ii.153-54) and "to profane the precious time" (II.iv.390-95). The echoes emphasize the *appearance* of his behavior from the beginning of *I Henry IV* to his turning point, signaled by "Falstaff, good night," in *II Henry IV*; in reality Hal has told us that his loose behavior has been deliberately planned as a foil of "sullen ground" to set off the "bright metal" of his "reformation" (*I Henry IV*, I.ii.231-40). Thus Hal redeems the time in an unusual way, by not walking circumspectly, by seeming to be a fool and not wise, while actually he is making "offence a skill" (I.ii.240).[6]

5. This interpretation, one that the allusions support, is markedly different from Bryant's, who sees Othello as a type of God. Although I cannot agree with Frye's condemnation of Bryant's view as absurd (*Shakespeare*, pp. 30-31), I believe Bryant would have been spared Frye's sarcasm if he had followed the Folio instead of the Quarto in the passage, though his "theologizing" analysis irks Frye.

6. Bryant, *Hippolyta's View*, Chapter Four; see also Jorgensen, " 'Redeeming Time' in Shakespeare's *Henry IV*," especially his emphasis on Hal's method of redeeming time, similar to that advocated in a contemporary sermon (p. 106).

How well Hal has paved the way for his change he shows when he becomes Henry V. Then the most authoritative English ecclesiastic, the Archbishop of Canterbury, finds him "full of grace and fair regard" (I.i.22). The language alludes to the Biblical description of the coming of Christ. "And the same woorde became fleash, and dwelt among us (and we saw the glorie of it, as the glorie of the only begotten sonne [that came] from the father), ful of grace and trueth" (John 1:14). The Archbishop, of course, has not forgotten the recent course of Henry's life. He says of Hal that at the very moment of Henry IV's death,

> Consideration like an angel came
> And whipp'd the offending Adam out of him,
> Leaving his body as a paradise
> T'envelop and contain celestial spirits.
> *(Henry V*, I.i.28-31; cf. Gen. 3:24)

One of the early scenes in *Henry V* shows Henry objective, swift and stern in his judgments. Having asked the traitors Gray, Scroop, and Cambridge what to do about a malefactor, and having heard their reasons against mercy, Henry reveals his knowledge of their treachery. When they appeal to his mercy, he says:

> The mercy that was quick in us but late,
> By your own counsel is suppress'd and kill'd.
> You must not dare, for shame, to talk of mercy,
> For your own reasons turn into your bosoms,
> As dogs upon their masters, worrying you.   (II.ii.79-83)

The words are similar to those in the Apocrypha: "He sheweth no mercie to a man which is like himselfe, howe dare he aske forgeveness of his sinnes" (Ecclus. 28:4). Then, emphasizing the enormity of their crime, Henry says,

> If that same demon that hath gull'd thee thus
> Should with his lion gait walk the whole world
> He might return to vasty Tartar back,
> And tell the legions, "I can never win
> A soul so easy as that Englishman's."   (II.ii.121-25)

The Scriptural image of the devil "as a roaring Lion who walketh about, seeking whom he may devoure" (I Pet. 5:8) adds effectively to the portrayal of Henry as the Christian king. Allusion to the same in *I Henry IV* characterizes Hotspur as a hot-headed fire-eater. When told to deliver his prisoners to Henry IV, his reaction is: "An if the devil come and roar for them, I will not send them" (I.iii.125-26). But, significantly, Hotspur says this *after* Henry has made his exit. Thus many other factors of setting, action, language, and character are operating so that the same allusion will result in different effects at different times.

King Henry's last words to the traitors identify them with sinful Adam:

> I will weep for thee;
> For this revolt of thine, methinks, is like
> Another fall of man. Their faults are open.
> Arrest them to the answer of the law;
> And God acquit them of their practices. (II.ii.140-44)

There is here a reminiscence of the Biblical saying, "Some mens sinnes are open beforehande, halting before unto judgement, and in some they follow after" (I Tim. 5:24). The sins of these English traitors are open and go before them to the court of both human and divine justice.

King Henry V, however, becomes more human as the play progresses. Recall his talk with Williams, his soliloquy on ceremony, and especially his delightful courtship of Katherine. Still, in each situation, possibly excepting the last, he is the most highly serious and dignified of human beings. Disclaiming responsibility for the sins of those who die in battle for their king, he says, "Therefore should every soldier in the wars do as every sick man in his bed, wash every mote out of his conscience; and dying so, death is to him advantage" (IV.i.187-90). The reference to the Biblical mote as the smallest speck of sin is obvious; not so obvious is Henry's echo of Paul's saying, "For Christ is to me life, and death is to me advantage" (Phil. 1:21). What could be taken as a cynical or ironic comment adds instead, when the allusion is recognized, to the impression of Henry's piety. Although it is not the king's duty to bear the sins of his subjects, he is concerned for their eternal as well as their temporal welfare.

Passing in disguise among his soldiers on the night before the Battle of Agincourt, Henry has been impressed, partly by his conversation with Williams, partly by the sight of his sleeping men, with the vast difference that responsibility and ceremony place between a king and a common laborer. Along with the classical allusion, Henry's contrast of the peasant with the king recalls a similar contrast in Ecclesiastes. After naming the outward symbols of kingship—scepter, sword, crown, robe, throne—Henry continues:

> No, not all these, thrice-gorgeous Ceremony,
> Not all these, laid in bed majestical,
> Can sleep so soundly as the wretched slave,
> Who with a body fill'd and vacant mind
> Gets him to rest, cramm'd with distressful bread,[7]
> Never sees horrid night, the child of hell,
> But like a lackey from the rise to set
> Sweats in the eye of Phoebus, and all night
> Sleeps in Elysium. (IV.i.283-91)

The specific text is—"A labouring man sleepeth sweetely, whether it be little or muche that he eateth; but the abundance of the riche wil not suffer him to sleepe" (Eccles. 5:12). But the passage recalls the central theme of the whole book: the vanity of the feverish activity in which man engages "under the sun."

Immediately preceding the Battle of Agincourt, Henry is associated with the Biblical judge of Israel who won a battle against impossible odds. Like Gideon, he does not wish for more men. To Westmoreland's wish for ten thousand men from England, he replies:

> O, do not wish one more!
> Rather proclaim it, Westmoreland, through my host,
> That he which hath no stomach to this fight,
> Let him depart. (IV.iii.33-36)

Henry commands Westmoreland in the same way God commanded Gideon to "make a proclamation—If any man . . . be afearde, let him returne, and depart early from mount Gilead" (Judg. 7:3).[8]

7. See the following amusing labyrinth of learned comment on the phrase "distressful bread," identified as Biblical by some scholars: Harrison, *Introducing Shakespeare,* pp. 37-38; Heist, "Fulness of Bread," pp. 139-42; Parrott, "Fulness of Bread"; Harrison, "Distressful Bread." Harrison has the last word by explaining that in *Introducing Shakespeare* he intended his comment on this passage to parody the methods of Spurgeon, *Shakespeare's Imagery and What It Tells Us;* he cut short the "concatenation of comments" with the "regret that Learning should have been so misled by Levity." For suggestions of other Biblical allusions in the passage, see Noble, p. 186.

8. Henry's proclamation seems to me an unmistakable allusion to Gideon's proclamation. Bryant sees an interesting analogy between Falstaff and Gideon, p. 66. Frye, *Shakespeare,* p. 6, reacts to Bryant's comment by saying that "the time has surely come to call a halt." Yet the scene Bryant speaks of (especially *II Henry IV,* III.ii.258-320) might appear (to one used to thinking of Biblical parallels) to be an ironic travesty of the Gideon story.

54

Then, when the battle is won with less than thirty losses against ten thousand for the French, the king, like the Biblical leaders, ascribes the victory to God and proclaims death to anyone who boasts or takes the praise from God (IV.vii.119-21). As the psalmist says of Israel's victories, "In God we boast all the day long, and praise thy name for ever" (Ps. 44:8).

Prince Hamlet is, of course, far different from King Henry V. The Biblical allusions associated with Hamlet do not invite appreciation for a divine kingliness of character. Unlike the decisive man of action, whose fighting and loving are equally bold and successful, Hamlet's moody, philosophical soliloquies only gradually give way to action guided by providence. Two embittering facts the Danish prince has to face are the carnal weakness of his mother and the frustration of his love for Ophelia; others are the disloyalty of his "friends," Rosencrantz and Guildenstern, the treachery of Claudius, the tendency of his own nature to seek personal revenge instead of waiting to be used as Heaven's minister. These are emphasized by Biblical allusion, and Horatio, his only true friend, speaks words which intensify at the end of the play the impression of Hamlet as one who has earned the rest of Heaven.

Hamlet, having put on his "antic disposition," gives a clue to his disappointment with Ophelia as he talks to Polonius. The father has forbidden the daughter any longer to admit the prince as her suitor. After Ophelia describes the distraught and pitiable state in which Hamlet came to her chamber, however, Polonius sees his action as having been too hasty. Then the prince, with an allusion that Polonius seems not to understand but which a Biblically informed audience would, engages in the following dialogue with the old man.

Ham. O Jephthah, judge of Israel, what a treasure hadst thou!
Pol. What treasure had he, my lord?
Ham. Why,
        "One fair daughter, and no more,
        The which he loved passing well."
Pol. [Aside] Still on my daughter.
Ham. Am I not i' the right, old Jephthah?
Pol. If you call me Jephthah, my lord, I have a daughter that I love passing well.
Ham. Nay, that follows not. (II.ii.422-32)

The story of the judge of Israel who vowed that in return for victory in battle he would sacrifice to God whatever came first from his tent door, is told in Judges 11:30-40. The passage has been variously interpreted. Either Jephthah made a human sacrifice of his daughter (who was the first to greet him upon his return home) by actually killing her, or he devoted her to God by having her pledge a life of virginity and service to God. The latter interpretation seems to be supported by the daughter's request to be allowed two months in which to "goe up and downe upon the mountaines, and bewaile [her] virginitie" (Judg. 11:37) and by the statement that her father "did with her according to his vowe whiche he had vowed; and she knew no man" (Judg. 11:39). Either way, Hamlet's point is well made. It does not follow that Polonius loves his daughter if he is called Jephthah, for because of a foolish suspicion he has thwarted his daughter and Hamlet in their love for each other.[9] The allusion may, too, foreshadow the fate of Ophelia, for her father is indirectly responsible for her death; her grief over Polonius' order that she reject Hamlet's attentions, Hamlet's consequent rejection of her ("Get thee to a nunnery"), and her grief over the death of her father lead her to lunacy.

The son's disillusionment with his mother is more than matched in intensity by his idolization of his father. Both feelings are communicated in the scene in Gertrude's chamber. Showing her pictures of both the late King Hamlet and Claudius, Prince Hamlet says:

> This was your husband. Look you now what follows:
> Here is your husband, like a mildew'd ear,
> Blasting his wholesome brother. (III.iv.63-65)

The attractive manliness of King Hamlet has just been emphasized by classical allusions associating him with Hyperion, Jove, Mars, and Mercury; now the young Hamlet, wishing to reinforce the unworthiness of Claudius, identifies him with the "seven eares . . . withered, thinne, and blasted with the east winde" (Gen. 41:23) which, in the dream of Pharaoh, "devoured the seven good eares." Joseph's interpretation was that the withered ears represented years

9. That Polonius has been and continues to be foolish would hardly be missed by an audience that heard perhaps twice each year the sermon "Against Swearing and Perjury"; Jephthah was used as an example of a man who "of a foolish devotion . . . made a fond and unadvised oath" which he should not have kept. *Certain Sermons*, p. 45.

of famine which would completely exhaust the stocks of grain grown during seven good years. Hamlet's extremely bitter revulsion against the relationship into which his mother has entered is communicated by nothing more powerfully than by the reference to the mildewed ear as not merely "blasted with the east winde" as in Scripture, but as itself "Blasting his wholesome brother."

When the ghost enters Gertrude's chamber, only Hamlet can see him. Amazed by his actions and words, Gertrude asks her son, "Whereon do you look?" He answers,

> On him, on him! Look you, how pale he glares!
> His form and cause conjoin'd, preaching to stones,
> Would make them capable.   (III.iv.125-27)

As Jesus made his triumphal entry into Jerusalem, his disciples raised such an outcry that the Pharisees urged Jesus to quiet them. Jesus answered, "I tel you, that if these woulde holde their peace, then shal the stones crie immediately" (Luke 19:40). The allusion is also to Matt. 3:9, where John the Baptist warns the Pharisees not to pride themselves on having Abraham for their father, for "God is able of these stones to raise up children unto Abraham." Hamlet's brief allusion suggests his belief in the holiness of his cause as well as the hypocritical position of Gertrude; she is like the Pharisees, who can see no cause for concern. Further, if Hamlet is not stirred, he will be worse than a stone. The allusion helps prepare the way for Gertrude's words which come closer to a statement of repentance than anything she says in the play: "O Hamlet, thou has cleft my heart in twain" (156).

Claudius knows, and the audience knows because of his soliloquies and asides, how hollow and unsatisfying his victories are; but as far as Hamlet and Horatio know, the king is enjoying to the fullest a crown, a beautiful queen, and a sense of power over men and circumstances. One factor in making Hamlet a sympathetic character is that in his own mind he is the underdog and the audience sees him as such. As he put it, Claudius

> hath kill'd my king and whor'd my mother,
> Popp'd in between th' election and my hopes,
> Thrown out his angle for my proper life
> And with such cozenage.   (V.ii.64-67)

There is at the end of the play a hint of connection between Hamlet and the poor beggar Lazarus, who, although he had suffered many evil things in life, was carried "by the angels into Abrahams bosome" (Luke 16:22). Horatio, appropriately, speaks the words. "Good night, sweet prince,/ And flights of angels sing thee to thy rest!"[10] (V.ii.370-71). Evidence that the Elizabethan audience would certainly have responded to Horatio's "rest" and possibly to Hamlet's "the rest is silence" as designating Heaven is in the official sermon "An Exhortation Against the Fear of Death." A Christian's death is portrayed as leading to "rest, and endless quietness," to "quietness, rest, and everlasting joy"; a Christian should not fear death, "which sent Lazarus the poor miserable man by Angels anon unto Abrahams bosom, a place of rest."[11] In this brief sermon, Lazarus's translation "from troubles unto rest" in Abraham's bosom is referred to explicitly three times and implied four other times.

Anyone noting the allusion to Luke would also recall the other side of the story and identify Claudius with the rich man Dives, whose fate after death was to lift up his eyes in a place of torment. Thus the tragedy of Hamlet's end is mitigated not only by the Fortinbras scene, which gives the impression of life proceeding on its course, a course that will be much better for Denmark now that the rottenness has been purged away, but also by the Biblical allusion in the words of Horatio.

Although for purposes of this study I have placed King Claudius and Iago in the category of villains, it is not quite fair to Claudius, for he is, at least, sufficiently conscientious to realize the heinous nature of his crimes and to wish that he could be otherwise. Iago is not.

In his soliloquy in the third act, allusions associate Claudius with Cain in his murder of Abel, David in his adultery with the wife of Uriah, and Esau in his fruitless search for a place of repentance.

> O, my offence is rank, it smells to heaven;
> It hath the primal eldest curse upon't,
> A brother's murder. Pray can I not,
> Though inclination be as sharp as will.

10. For a discussion of Horatio's "rest" as a significant echo of Hamlet's "The rest is silence," see Elliott, *Scourge and Minister*, p. 205. Elliott notes also how far Romeo's dying pun on "rest" (*Romeo and Juliet*, V.iii.110) is "surpassed by the fine double-entendre in Hamlet's final speech" (p. 205). Sister Miriam Joseph, in "*Hamlet*, A Christian Tragedy," p. 136, has pointed out the parallel between Horatio's words and the Christian burial service: "In paradisum deducant te angeli. . . . Chorus angelorum te suscipiat." See also Frye, *Shakespeare*, pp. 135-36.

11. *Certain Sermons*, pp. 54, 61-62.

> My stronger guilt defeats my strong intent,
> And, like a man to double business bound,
> I stand in pause where I shall first begin,
> And both neglect. What if this cursed hand
> Were thicker than itself with brother's blood
> Is there not rain enough in the sweet heavens
> To wash it white as snow? (III.iii.36-46)

He remembers that Cain was condemned by God with the words: "And now art thou cursed from the earth, whiche hath opened her mouth to receive thy brothers blood from thy hande" (Gen. 4:11).[12] But when he asks, "Is there not rain enough in the sweet heavens/ To wash it white as snow?" the imagery is from David's psalm of repentance: "Thou shalt purge me with hysope, and I shalbe cleane: thou shalt washe me, and I shalbe whiter than snowe" (Ps. 51:7). Another phrase using the same imagery is "though your sinnes be as red as scarlet, they shalbe as white as snowe" (Isa. 1:18b).

Claudius's words and actions presently become associated with Esau, who "was reprobated: for he founde no place of repentance, though he sought it carefully with teares" (Heb. 12:17).

> What then? What rests?
> Try what repentance can. What can it not?
> Yet what can it when one cannot repent?
> (III.iii.64-66)

The king then kneels in an effort to make himself repent. But when he rises, like Esau he has sought, with desperation if not tears, a place of repentance and not found it. It is as a reprobate that he says,

> My words fly up, my thoughts remain below.
> Words without thoughts never to heaven go.
> (III.iii.97-98)

After this passage he never considers praying or penitence again.[13]

Of all Shakespeare's villains, Iago is perhaps the most unrelieved-

---

12. Bryant points out that Claudius inadvertently "links his dead brother . . . with the murdered Abel" (p. 119) by his earlier reference to the "common theme" of death that has cried out, "From the first corse till he that died today,/ This must be so!" (I.ii.103-6).

13. For a similar allusion in Milton's *Paradise Lost*, IV, connecting Satan with Esau in the soliloquy that concludes "Evil, be thou my good" see Sims, *The Bible in Milton's Epics*, pp. 174-75. Milton probably had both the Bible's Esau and Shakespeare's Claudius in mind; his dramatic uses of the Bible in *P.L.* owe much to Shakespeare.

ly Satanic; no flavor of sweetness nor spark of light mitigates the Stygian blackness of his depravity.[14] In characterizing this villain, Shakespeare used Biblical allusion in much the same way as he used it for other characters in other plays; in addition, however, he used Biblical reversals, of the Marlovian type. These reversals will be considered in the last section of this chapter.

In the opening scene Roderigo wonders why Iago will follow the Moor if he hates him. Iago answers:

> O, sir, content you;
> I follow him to serve my turn upon him.
> We cannot all be masters, nor all masters
> Cannot be truly follow'd. (I.i.41-44)

Since masters have a greater responsibility for their actions than servants, Christian brethren should not have the desire to be "many maisters, knowing howe that we shal receive the greater damnation" (Jas. 3:1). Iago plans to see to it that the Bible warning is fulfilled and that his master shall receive the greater damnation.

"I am not what I am" (I.i.65), Iago says, in direct contrast with the apostle Paul, who said, "I am what I am" (I Cor. 15:10a). How smoothly he can belie appearance soon becomes evident as he tells Othello of his encounter with Brabantio. "I lack iniquity/ Sometimes to do me service" (I.ii.3-4), he says, and then,

> Nay, but he prated,
> And spoke such scurvy and provoking terms
> Against your honour
> That, with the little godliness I have,
> I did full hard forbear him. (I.ii.6-10)

Iago pretends to have lived up to the Biblical injunction about "forbearing one another in love" (Eph. 4:2) and "forbearing one another, and forgeving one another, if any man have a quarel against any" (Col. 3:13).

When Othello charges him on pain of death to prove Desdemona's infidelity, Iago puts on the part of the honest man who has been a fool to try to help his friend. To be honest is not safe, he says, and he thanks Othello for teaching him this lesson.

14. See Spivack, *Shakespeare and the Allegory of Evil*, p. 3, where Iago is associated with the Biblical phrase "the mystery of iniquity" (II Thess. 2:7). See also West, "Iago and the Mystery of Iniquity," for an extension of the train of thought begun by Spivack's association of Iago's evil and Paul's words.

Oth.   Nay, stay. Thou shouldst be honest.
Iago.   I should be wise, for honesty's a fool
     And loses that it works for.   (III.iii.381-83)

In the parable of the unjust steward, who through dishonesty made provision for his future when he was discharged, the master "commended the unjust stewarde, because he had donne wisely; for the children of this world, are in their nation wiser than the children of light" (Luke 16:8). Iago is like the unjust steward who took advantage of his master; and, like the master in the parable, Othello is soon commending his trusted servant, though unwittingly, for his injustice to himself and to his wife.

The allusion which perhaps bests sums up the character of Iago is used by his wife. As Othello questions Emilia about Desdemona, Emilia gives passionately earnest utterance to her faith in Desdemona.

     I durst, my lord, to wager she is honest,
     Lay down my soul at stake. If you think other,
     If any wretch have put this in your head,
     Let Heaven requite it with the serpent's curse!
                           (IV.ii.12-15)

The identification of Iago with the serpent who was "cursed above all cattel, and above every beast of the feelde" (Gen. 3:14) provides the first opportunity in the play for someone other than Iago to say about him what needs saying; and though Emilia and Othello do not yet make the connection, the audience or the reader can feel only sympathy for the indignation of Emilia.

Although no example has been discovered of Shakespeare's repeating a Biblical motif throughout a play for the purpose of unifying the play[15]—such a repetition as appears in *Eastward Ho!* for example—he uses Biblical allusion to underscore and emphasize the theme of a play and to anticipate the future line of action. An example of the latter is Benvolio's command to the servants of the Capulets and Montagues as they quarrel on the streets of Verona. It is true of all four servants but especially Sampson and Gregory (representing the Capulets) that they wish no part of a violent conflict; they merely draw to impress Tybalt. Benvolio immediately

15. Bryant, pp. 52-67, makes a claim very near this for the allusion to Ephesians in *I* and *II Henry IV*, but contrasts between old and new seem, like contrasts between light and darkness, too commonplace in non-Christian as well as Christian contexts to make a case.

61

beats down their swords and commands, "Put up your swords; you know not what you do" (I.i.72). These words, when remembered later, take on increasing significance as the plot develops. They are reminiscent of the words of Christ: "Father, forgeve them, for they wote not what they doo" (Luke 23:34). True, the servants know not what they are doing, but, even more ironically, Benvolio knows not what he is initiating. The hot-headed Tybalt appears, finds Benvolio drawn among the servants, tries to kill him, and the result is that the Capulet-Montague feud breaks into new flame. Nothing in the unfolding of the plot depends on the Biblical phrase, but if it is remembered, the dramatic irony of good intentions gone awry is intensified.

One theme of *Romeo and Juliet,* that the lovers are "star-cross'd" and that theirs is a "death-mark'd love," is stated in the prologue. Such paradoxes as are also stated in the prologue—e.g., that only through the children's death can the rage of the feuding parents against one another be removed—are underscored by Biblical allusion. Romeo and Friar Laurence give utterance to the theme of paradox most frequently, but it is also involved in the speech of Juliet (as when she calls Romeo "wolvish ravening lamb" and fiend incarnate in a "paradise of flesh" [III.ii.76, 83]). Speaking of the coldness of his beloved Rosaline towards him, Romeo says:

> Why, then, O brawling love! O loving hate!
> O anything, of nothing first create!
> O heavy lightness! serious vanity!
> Mis-shapen chaos of well-seeming forms!
> Feather of lead, bright smoke, cold fire, sick health!
> Still-waking sleep, that is not what it is!
> This love feel I, that feel no love in this.   (I.i.182-88)

Embedded in this cluster of paradoxes is the traditional interpretation of creation as a making of anything and everything *ex nihilo* (Gen. 1:1, Heb. 11:3); although it is only one paradox among many, it ironically anticipates his coming fall into love with a girl of the family of his enemies.

The paradox that immoderate love will lead to tragedy is emphasized by Biblical allusion. Friar Laurence warns Romeo:

> The sweetest honey
> Is loathsome in his own deliciousness
> And in the taste confounds the appetite;
> Therefore love moderately.   (III.vi.11-14)

Such is the temperance urged by the wise man of the Book of Proverbs: "If thou findest honie, eate so much as is sufficient for thee; lest thou be over ful, and parbreake it out againe. . . . He that is ful, abhorreth an hony combe: but unto him that is hungry, every fowle thing is sweete" (Prov. 25:15, 27:7).

Upon his first appearance in the play, Friar Laurence, who is vitally instrumental in the development of the plot, describes nature in paradoxical terms.

> The grey-ey'd morn smiles on the frowning night,
> Chequ'ring the eastern clouds with streaks of light,
> And flecked darkness *like a drunkard reels*
> From forth day's path and Titan's fiery wheels.
>
> (II.iii.1-4; italics added)

Biblical imagery is echoed in the italicized phrase; "the earth shal *reele to and fro like a drunkarde*, & shalbe removed like a tent, and the iniquities thereof shalbe beaten upon it, it shal falle, and not rise up againe" (Isa. 24:20; italics added). The Friar goes on to refer to earth as both the womb and the tomb of life, bringing forth both life-giving herbs and death-dealing drugs; the Biblical image coupled with the paradoxes of the passage suggest both that tragedy is impending and that ultimate good will come out of it. Referring to a flower whose scent cheers but whose taste will kill, Friar Laurence says,

> Two such opposed kings encamp them still
> In man as well as herbs, grace and rude will;
> And where the worser is predominant,
> Full soon the canker death eats up that plant.
>
> (II.iii.27-30)

The idea of sin (which results from the will) and grace as opposing kings reigning within man originates in the New Testament explanation of man's fall through Adam and of man's redemption through Christ: "That as sinne hathe reined unto death, even so might grace reign through righteousnesse unto eternal life by Jesus Christ oure Lord" (Rom. 5:21).

The paradoxical notion of good springing from what seems only evil is at the heart of the play; the woe of the story of "Juliet and her Romeo" is not lessened, but the point is made that "fate," "the stars," or "Heaven" directed affairs for a good end in spite of the

63

tragedy. The Prince says to Montague and Capulet as they stand over the dead bodies of their children: "See, what a scourge is laid upon your hate,/ That Heaven finds means to kill your joys with love"[16] (V.iii.292-93; cf. I John 4:18).

Two Biblical allusions in *Hamlet* occur at a crucial point to foreshadow action and add dramatic force to the reasons given by the prince for his actions. At the close of the second act Hamlet is planning the "Mousetrap" play; he has already been assured of his uncle's guilt, but he fears that the Ghost's testimony may be a trick of Satan:

> The spirit that I have seen
> May be the devil; and the devil hath power
> T'assume a pleasing shape; yea, and perhaps
> Out of my weakness and my melancholy,
> As he is very potent with such spirits,
> Abuses me to damn me. (II.ii.627-32)

The explanation is sufficient motivation, on the face of it, for Hamlet to seek confirmation of Claudius's guilt. For an audience familiar with the Bible, however, the words have added force, since the New Testament warns that "Satan himselfe is transfourmed into an angel of light" (II Cor. 11:14). Known also to the Elizabethans who were familiar with either the Bishops' or the Genevan version was the marginal note (I Sam. 28:14), explaining that Samuel's spirit appeared only to Saul's "imagination, albeit it was Satan, who to blinde his eyes tooke upon him the forme of Samuel, as he can do of an Angel of light."[17] The only reasonable course for Hamlet to follow, therefore, is to test the truth of the ghost's statement.

That Hamlet has not been convinced that the spirit is his father's is emphasized again in the opening of the third act. In his "To be or not to be" soliloquy, Hamlet asks if anyone would endure the unhappiness of life were it not for dread

> of something after death,
> The undiscover'd country from whose bourn
> No traveller returns. (III.i.78-80)

He has, of course, talked with one who represents himself as a

16. See Siegel, "Christianity and the Religion of Love in *Romeo and Juliet*," especially pp. 387-89.
17. Noble, p. 203.

traveler from the undiscovered country, but he distrusts that one. His own conviction, that travelers do not return from that land, has the authority of Scripture behind it in such passages as "the way that I must goe is at hande, from whence I shal not turne againe" (Job 16:22) and "neither is there any man knowen to have returned from the grave" (Wisd. 2:1). After the play within the play Hamlet, having seen the stricken look of Claudius as the player king is poisoned, says to Horatio, "I'll take the ghost's word for a thousand pound" (III.ii.297). His conviction that Claudius is guilty is all the stronger and all the more dramatically persuasive because of his initial reluctance to believe the ghost, a reluctance based on Scripture.[18]

One theme of the play, several times reiterated, is that divine Providence guides in the affairs of men; near the end, Hamlet utters the idea in clearly Biblical terms, and his earlier utterances involve oblique Biblical allusion. For example, having seen the ghost for the first time and learned of his uncle's crime, Hamlet says, "The time is out of joint;—O cursed spite,/ That ever I was born to set it right!" (I.v.189-90). His belief that his birth was for a specific purpose echoes Christ's "To this ende was I borne" (John 19:37). In Gertrude's chamber he hesitates not at all to kill the person behind the arras, though he thinks it is the king. Finding that it is instead Polonius, he says,

18. Bryant contends, "As far as Hamlet is concerned, the Gonzago play proves only that Claudius murdered his father. He does not stop to ask whether it proves the authority of the ghost as well" (p. 128). Yet it seems to me that Hamlet's confidence in the ghost's word (III.ii.297) reflects also his acceptance of the ghost's authority as a divinely commissioned messenger. Bryant's view leads him to identify the prayer scene as the climax of the action and to say that Hamlet should have killed the king while he was praying (p. 129). Several years earlier, Elliott had given the same answer in *Scourge and Minister* (p. 109). Bowers has, I think, conclusively settled this point, not so much in his "Hamlet as Minister and Scourge," as in his "Dramatic Structure and Criticism: Plot in *Hamlet*," pp. 207-18. He demonstrates that in terms of plot structure the climax must be the closet scene in which Hamlet kills Polonius, thus initiating the action that will lead to the joining of Claudius and Laertes. The parallel Bowers draws between Hamlet and Milton's Samson is convincing to me. See also Bowers, "Death in Victory"; Sister Miriam Joseph, pp. 110-40. She agrees with Elliott and Bryant that the turning point of the play is the prayer scene and that Hamlet should have killed the king, though only with a "conscientious right-seeking mind" concerned for the king's salvation (p. 133). Bowers argues, "If a tragic flaw in a sympathetic character is to be pinpointed as his refusal to kill a defenseless man at prayer, then the English dramatic hero was modelled on the tradition of the Renaissance Italian villain, a patently absurd proposition" ("Dramatic Structure," pp. 212-13).

> For this same lord,
> I do repent; but Heaven hath pleas'd it so,
> To punish me with this and this with me,
> That I must be their scourge and minister.
>
> (III.iv.172-75)

Hamlet is sorry to have killed Polonius but he recognizes the hand of God. Heaven has now punished him with a wrong corpse that results from his vengeful thrust; as a scourge he has punished Polonius. Now he sees that he must be *"their* scourge and minister" (italics mine). Not simply Polonius but also Claudius, Rosencrantz, Guildenstern, and the entire rottenness of Denmark represented by such a king and such a counselor as Polonius must suffer the vengeance of God at the hand of "the minister of God, a revenger to execute wrath upon him that doeth evil" (Rom. 13:4).[19]

Even Hamlet's indiscretion sometimes serves him well, because "There's a divinity that shapes our ends,/ Roughhew them how we will" (V.ii.10-11). The idea expressed is Scriptural, although the language is not; for example, Proverbs states "A man deviseth a way in his heart; but it is the Lord that ordereth his goings" (Prov. 16:9). Thus the theme of God's providence in directing Hamlet's life and actions is reiterated throughout the play, both with and without Biblical allusion. But the final example is unquestionably Biblical.

Immediately before the duel with Laertes, Hamlet has a premonition of disaster but rejects Horatio's suggestion that the duel be called off. He says: "Not a whit; we defy augury. There's a special providence in the fall of a sparrow. If it be now, 'tis not to come; if it be not to come, it will be now; if it be not now, yet it will come; the readiness is all" (V.ii.230-34). The allusion recalls the words of Jesus: "Are not two sparrowes sold for a farthing, and one of them shal not fall on the ground without your Father?" (Matt. 10:29).[20] Although it may not be confidently asserted as Shakespeare's belief, it can surely be taken as Hamlet's belief that the affairs of men are ordered by Heaven. From his point of view the final scene, rather than "accidental judgements, casual slaughters" as Horatio sees it, is a careful pattern of justice. Gertrude, for whom Claudius poisoned her husband, is poisoned by wine pre-

19. See Bowers' three articles just cited.
20. Shakespeare alludes to the Genevan version here; the Bishops' Bible has "light on the grounde" for "fall on the ground."

pared by Claudius; Laertes is killed by his own treachery; Claudius is killed by a sword he poisoned for Hamlet and by being forced to drink the poisoned wine he had prepared for Hamlet; even Hamlet dies justly, for Laertes, whose father Hamlet killed, kills Hamlet. That there is a special providence in the fall of each of those who die in the last scene is felt by the reader or spectator. Towards this the statements of Hamlet on predestination, and especially the clear Biblical allusion involved in the last of those statements, have been building.[21]

Although Shakespeare at times uses Biblical allusion with a significant reversal, as Marlowe did before him, the dramatic effects which result are often quite different from Marlowe's.

The process by which Shakespeare has derived from Marlowe a certain type of character and a distinctive rhetoric but has entirely new-created them to his own purpose is outlined by Nicholas Brooke.[22] And that purpose, says Brooke, is, "radically unlike Marlowe, the final identification of the Machiavel with an orthodox conception of evil." That is, Marlowe's ethos is essentially alien to Shakespeare and he assimilated it with difficulty "through a process of imitative re-creation merging into critical parody." After *Julius Caesar*, Brooke maintains, the assimilation is complete; dependence on Marlowe is never shown, though reference to order is always asserted with simple confidence but with a complex of disturbing recognitions. Now something akin to this process may be true of Shakespeare's reversals in Biblical allusion. Marlowe's method of emphasizing a violation of order by alluding to divine order at the very moment when it is being broken, as in *Faustus* and *The Jew*, may dimly appear in *Romeo and Juliet*, *Hamlet*, *Othello*, and *King Lear*; but it seems to me that Shakespeare's usage is never so clear-cut, never so one-purposed as Marlowe's. Shakespeare's reversals are "Marlovian" only in being reversals; the effects are myriad. Where Marlowe reversed the roles of his speakers, the values of the passages alluded to, or the meaning of the passages to impress the viewer, or reader, with the blasphemous violation of normal Christian order achieved by a Faustus or a Barabas, Shakespeare's reversals must be identified in terms of different effects rather than

21. See Bowers, "The Moment of Final Suspense in *Hamlet:* We Defy Augury." On Horatio's point of view as Shakespeare's view, see J. V. Cunningham, *Tradition and Poetic Structure*, pp. 158-63.

22. "Marlowe as Provocative Agent in Shakespeare's Early Plays," pp. 38, 44.

of different methods of reversal. To oversimplify: Marlowe uses various kinds of reversal of Scripture to achieve a single effect; Shakespeare achieves a variety of effects by Marlovian methods of reversal and by other methods peculiarly his own. Shakespearean reversals add humor to an already funny situation and make a serious point, as in both parts of *Henry IV*; they emphasize the blackness of a sin or the villainy of a sinner, as in *Hamlet* and *Othello*; and they deepen the pathos of human tragedy, as in *King Lear*.

Falstaff, seeking to persuade Prince Hal to "practice an answer" for his father when he is called before the king, pretends to be King Henry IV and gives Hal advice about the kind of company he keeps. In the midst of a passage of euphuistic mock-seriousness, Falstaff says: "There is a thing, Harry, which thou hast often heard of and it is known to many in our land by the name of pitch. This pitch, as ancient writers do report, doth defile; so doth the company that thou keepest; for, Harry, now I do not speak to thee in drink but in tears; not in pleasure but in passion, not in words only, but in woes also; and yet there is a virtuous man whom I have often noted in thy company, but I know not his name" (II.iv.452-61). One of the "ancient writers" who refer to pitch is the author of Ecclesiasticus, who says: "Who so toucheth pitch, shalbe defiled withal: and he that is familier with the proude, shal clothe himselfe with pride. He taketh a burthen upon him that accompanieth a more honorable manne than him selfe, therefore keepe no familiaritie with one that is richer than thee" (Ecclus. 13:1-2). Falstaff, speaking as Hal's father, warns the prince against defiling company with allusion to a passage which is aimed more at one like Falstaff himself than at Hal.[23] The "virtuous man" Falstaff wants to exclude from the pitch category is, of course, himself; but he is disobeying the command that he "keepe no familiaritie with one that is richer

23. Reaction to Falstaff's knowledge and use of the Bible ranges from such neutral remarks as Spurgeon's "it is certain from his language that he knows his Bible well," *Shakespeare's Imagery*, p. 378, to Bowden's assertion that in Falstaff Shakespeare was satirizing Oldcastle, "one of the Protestant heroes of the day . . . to manifest his sympathies with the ancient faith," *Religion of Shakespeare*, pp. 144-45. Bowden even refers to "Shakespeare's portrait of Falstaff as a Puritan and sanctimonious hypocrite" (p. 138), and he lumps Sir John with Angelo, Shallow, and Malvolio! Though De Groot attempts also to prove Shakespeare a Catholic, he is moderately noncommittal on Falstaff, merely reporting that he "is accused by some of being a backsliding Puritan" (*The Shakespeares*, p. 168).

than thee," a command that appears in the context of the passage
on pitch he is alluding to. The Lyly-like rhetoric, with its alliteration and parallelism, is even more hilarious if it is recognized that
Falstaff is trying to make a point by allusion to a text which emphasizes the reverse of his point.[24]

As Falstaff, still impersonating the king, defends Falstaff, an allusion to a much more familiar passage occurs. "If then the tree may
be known by the fruit, as the fruit by the tree, then, peremptorily
I speak it, there is virtue in that Falstaff; him keep with, the rest
banish" (II.iv.470-73). The Biblical statement is actually that "every tree is knowen by his owne fruite" (Luke 6:44). Falstaff's argument is that Falstaff looks virtuous; the Bible says that the fruit
may be known by the tree; conversely, then, the tree may be known
by its fruit; its fruit is a virtuous appearance; *ergo*, the tree is virtuous. To use the Biblical text properly, however, he would have to
state his syllogism differently. The tree may be known by its fruit;
conversely, the fruit may be known by the appearance of the tree;
the tree appears virtuous, therefore the fruit must be good. This
reversal involves the kind of hair-splitting distinction upon which
so many Elizabethan puns turn. Certainly to a modern audience,
thoroughly familiar with roly-poly, white-bearded Santa Claus,
Falstaff's looks would belie his morals, and such a figure was attractive to the Elizabethans without the benefit of the jolly Saint Nick
of the modern Christmastime.[25] That the fat man of Shakespeare's
plays was loved in spite of, as well as because of, his rascality certainly needs no better testimony than that Queen Elizabeth I should
desire that he be resurrected for *The Merry Wives of Windsor*.
Such a fat man makes a not very convincing villain, and "everybody loves a fat man" is not a proverb coined recently. As Falstaff
himself puts it, with another reversal of Biblical allusion, "If to be

24. The effect of such allusions goes further than simply to add humor; see
Small, "The Reflective Element in Falstaff," who argues that the use of Biblical allusion is one way Shakespeare has of making us sympathize with, and see
the "serious underbelly" of, Falstaff's humor. He concludes, "Shakespeare uses
this serious strain in Falstaff to enhance the humorous side of his character. But
critics are agreed that the character of Falstaff is not entirely accounted for by
saying that his mind is made up of a combination of the rogue, jester and gull"
(p. 143). The similar effect of reversals of allusion to Scripture has not, I think,
been noted before.

25. However, the fat Sir John with a cushion on his head for a crown
(II.iv.416-17) might well be recognized by Elizabethans as a living emblem
of lechery. Chew, *The Virtues Reconciled*, pp. 15-17.

fat be to be hated, then Pharoah's lean kine are to be loved" (II.iv. 519-20). The "seven other kine . . . poore and very il favoured and leane fleashed" of Pharoah's dream (Gen. 41:19) were never loved by anyone who read about them.

Also in *I Henry IV* the prince has himself been guilty of reversing Scripture in its purpose. In answer to Falstaff's statement that an old lord of the council had talked to him about Hal very wisely in the street but that Falstaff had not regarded him, Hal says, "Thou didst well; for wisdom cries out in the streets, and no man regards it" (I.ii.99-100). This is an almost exact quotation of "Wisedome crieth without and putteth foorth voice in the streetes . . . and no man regarded" (Prov. 1:20, 24). Hal takes the passage out of context as though it stated a condition that should exist, thus reversing its meaning. Perhaps the most humorous effect is the reaction from Falstaff: "O, thou hast damnable iteration and art indeed able to corrupt a saint. Thou hast done much harm upon me, Hal; God forgive thee for it!" (I.ii.101-3). This statement, particularly the phrase "damnable iteration" (meaning the quotation of Scripture for an unholy use), is especially appreciated by those who observe Shakespeare's own reversed use of the Bible.[26]

Mrs. Quickly, the hostess, who used malapropisms long before Mrs. Malaprop, gets off, unwittingly, a ludicrous "damnable iteration" in a conversation with Doll Tearsheet. The Bible refers to woman as the "weaker vessel" (I Pet. 3:7) and urges that those "whiche are strong ought to beare the infirmities of the weake" (Rom. 15:1).[27] Speaking of Falstaff, Mrs. Quickly says to Doll (in *II Henry IV*): "You cannot bear with another's confirmities. What the good-year! One must bear, and that must be you; you are the weaker vessel, as they say, the emptier vessel" (II.iv.63-66). Although Doll would hardly recognize that Mrs. Quickly has turned the Biblical text upside down and confused it with another, she has common sense enough to see what is wrong with the logic of the weaker bearing the stronger. She asks, "Can a weak empty vessel bear such a huge full hogshead?" (II.iv.67).

The blackness of a sin or the villainy of a sinner can be greatly emphasized by ironic reversals of Biblical statements, as Shake-

26. A similar "damnable iteration" is used by Hamlet when he proves from Scripture that Claudius is his mother: "Father and mother is man and wife, man and wife is one flesh, and so, my mother" (IV.iii.53-55; Gen. 2:24).

27. Another use by Shakespeare of the Genevan version; instead of "infirmities" the Bishops' Bible has "fraylenesse."

speare demonstrates in the speeches of Hamlet, Othello, Iago, and Cordelia.[28]

As Hamlet, figuratively, sets up a looking glass in which to show his mother "the inmost part" of herself (III.iv.19, 20), she varies in her reaction from indignation, through fear, to remorse. What I have called, in the discussion of Marlowe, the looking-glass view of Scripture is used effectively in the speech of Hamlet to bring his mother to such a sense of overpowering conviction and shame that she can do little more than beg him to speak no more. In the same speech containing the Biblical image of Claudius as a "mildew'd ear,/ Blasting his wholesome brother," Hamlet cries out to Gertrude, "O shame! where is thy blush?" (III.iv.82). Though the words used are not the same, the structure is that of familiar rhetorical questions from Scripture: "O Death where is thy sting: O hel where is thy victory?" (I Cor. 15:55). The apostle Paul asks these questions in triumph; the implied answer is that the sting of death and the victory of the grave (Hades) have been abolished by Christ. Hamlet reverses the implied answer to make it signal the defeat of virtue in Gertrude. As the Biblical question proclaims victory over the consequences of evil, Hamlet's question ironically proclaims victory over moral virtue; if the matron Gertrude can sin without shame, "Proclaim no shame" to all sinners, says her son. Before this speech of Hamlet's, Gertrude has been asking, "What have I done?" and "Ay me, what act,/ That roars so loud and thunders in the index?" (III.iv.52-53). After this speech the Queen says,

> O Hamlet, speak no more!
> Thou turn'st mine eyes into my very soul,
> And there I see such black and grained spots
> As will not leave their tinct.   (III.iv.88-91)

She has beheld herself in a glass (Jas. 1:23; III.iv.19-20); Hamlet has accomplished his purpose, and at least part of his success (as well as Shakespeare's success in making the scene so effective and Gertrude's sin heinous even in her own eyes) results from the looking glass of Scripture.

Othello, in the bedchamber murder scene, uses the exact words,

28. Sharpe, in Chapter V of his *Irony in the Drama*, analyzes Shakespeare's development as a playwright in terms of his development as an ironist. The specific evidence of ironic use of Biblical allusion supports Sharpe's generalizations.

as well as the structure, of the Bible when he says to Desdemona, "Peace and be still!" (V.ii.47). Jesus himself used these words in the Gospel story of his calming the storm on the Sea of Galilee; Othello uses them to command Desdemona to silence. Jesus's words, "Peace, and be stil" (Mark 4:39) immediately brought calm to the wind and the waves; these words, used by Jesus to save lives, are used by Othello, himself a tempest of "bloody passion" (V.ii.44), to quiet the one whose life he intends to take. The ironic reversal stresses the vengeful, certainly un-Christlike[29] (though he is thinking of himself as a righteous avenger) mood of Othello as well as the fear and agitation of Desdemona. For one who recognizes the Biblical source of Othello's imperative, the dramatic irony of the scene is increased to almost unbearable intensity. Othello thinks of himself as a priest about to make a sacrifice (V.ii.65) and his use of Christ's words underscores, simultaneously, both Othello's mistaken notion of his role and the pathos of Desdemona's plight—she is as powerless to resist Othello, her lord, as the wind and the waves of Galilee were to resist the Lord of Nature.[30]

Iago is a Barabas-like villain who has reversed traditional Christian values and devoted himself to an evil course; he himself calls his reasoning "Divinity of hell!" (II.iii.356). With the dissimulation of a Marlovian Machiavel, Iago uses good to bring forth evil and to make out of Desdemona's "own goodness . . . the net/ That shall enmesh them all" (II.iii.367-68). Othello trusts him; Cassio trusts him; Desdemona trusts him. Cassio speaks for all the people Iago works against when he says, never suspecting Iago of treachery, "I never knew/ A Florentine more kind and honest" (III.i.43-44). One dramatic device Shakespeare uses to make his villain constantly blacker is reversed Biblical allusion.

In the soliloquy near the end of the second act, having set in motion the mills of evil that grind through the rest of the play, Iago says that Othello so loves Desdemona that he will do anything for her, even "were't to renounce his baptism,/ All seals and symbols

29. For a discussion of Othello as particularly prone to sexual jealousy see Rossiter, "Othello: A Moral Essay," in *Angel With Horns*, pp. 189-208. If his view is sound, it follows that Othello is not only un-Christlike, he is Iago-like, else Iago could not have wrought him to this extreme.

30. Had Bryant noted this allusion to the words of Christ, he would doubtless have considered it a reinforcement of his view of Othello as a representation of divinity, perhaps even of God. However, the important dimension here is the reversal by which our horror at Othello's presumption of the office of minister of vengeance is increased.

72

of redeemed sin" (II.iii.349-50). The allusion is to a Bible verse
which warns, "And greeve not the holy spirite of God, by whome
ye are sealed unto the day of redemption" (Eph. 4:30). If this
statement and its allusion are remembered in the last scene when
Othello speaks of Desdemona's gaze which will cause him to be
hurled from the judgment seat of God into "steep-down gulfs of
liquid fire" (V.ii.280), the full effect of the irony of the reversal is
evident. Desdemona does not seek to influence Othello to renounce
the seals of his redemption, but the image of an unfaithful Desdemona, placed in Othello's mind by Iago, causes him to murder her
and renounce his own salvation.

Having placed nebulous doubts in Othello's mind about the relationship between Cassio and Desdemona, and pretending reluctance to air his thoughts about Cassio, Iago subtly brings in a
reference to Desdemona without naming her when he says, "Good
name in man and woman, dear my lord,/ Is the immediate jewel of
their souls" (III.iii.155-56). Although he immediately launches into
the oft-quoted lines beginning "Who steals my purse steals trash,"
Iago's intention is to steal the good name of Cassio—and of Desdemona. The allusion to Scripture makes his purpose seem all the
more honest to Othello while it makes him the greater traitor to the
audience. "A good name is more to be desired than great riches:
and loving favour [is better] then silver and golde" (Prov. 22:1).

There are times in *King Lear* when Cordelia's character is made
more sympathetic by Biblical allusion. For example, when she is
asked how much she loves her father, her answer may seem, even
to the audience, to be lacking in warmth and affection. Even though
she is disgusted at the hypocrisy of her sisters, she should be able
to express honestly her love for Lear, one feels, and thus avoid his
wrath. If one realizes however, that she is acting in accord with
the advice of the Bible, her words have more of an affectionate
connotation and one can appreciate the difficulty of her position.
She says,

> Unhappy that I am, I cannot heave
> My heart into my mouth. I love your Majesty
> According to my bond; no more nor less.   (I.i.93-95)

The Bible commands such an attitude: "The hart of fooles is in
their mouth: but the mouth of the wise is in their hart" (Ecclus.
21:26). Although Cordelia may have the outward appearance of

73

foolish stubbornness and the sisters seem wise, the evoked passage indicates exactly the opposite.

Cordelia's parting words to Goneril and Regan involve a sarcastic reversal of Biblical statement. Knowing that their expressed love is not sincere, Cordelia says,

> Time shall unfold what plighted cunning hides;
> Who covers faults, at last shame them derides.
> Well may you prosper! (I.i.283-85)

The last line wishes, ironically, for the sisters what the Bible makes clear they will not have: "He that hideth his sinnes, shal not prosper: but whoso knowledgeth them, and forsaketh them, shal have mercy" (Prov. 28:13). The allusion emphasizes, before the play has revealed by action, the sinful and hypocritical natures of the older sisters, and it foreshadows the end of those who seem at first to prosper.

Many tragic experiences must be suffered before the wrongs of the beginning of *King Lear* are righted, however; the central sufferer is, of course, Lear himself. Reversals of Scripture in his speech stress the important lessons that are revealed to him in his exile and exposure.[31] Although he is mad, dressed fantastically in wild flowers, Lear knows, finally, that a king is still a human being who, though he may command men, cannot command nature—or even himself, if his passions rule him. When, near the end, he meets Gloucester and Edgar, Lear rambles on with his "Reason in madness," as Edgar calls it. "Ha! Goneril, with a white beard! They flatter'd me like a dog, and told me I had the white hairs in my beard ere the black ones were there. To say 'ay' and 'no' to everything that I said! 'Ay' and 'no' too was no good divinity. When the rain came to wet me once, and the wind to make me chatter; when the thunder would not peace at my bidding; there I smelt 'em out. Go to, they are not men o' their words: they told me I was everything: 'tis a lie, I am not ague-proof" (IV.vi.97-107). Lear now realizes that his retinue, except for Kent whom he banished, was made up of yes-men and no-men. Such "aye" and "no" flattering was not good theology, he says, for it made him think he was omnipotent

---

31. Some humorous allusions occur in Lear's speech. He says to the ragged Edgar, "I do not like the fashion of your garments: you will say they are Persian; but let them be chang'd" (III.vi.84-86), alluding to the ancient laws of the Medes and Persians which were not to be changed (Dan. 6:8). See Noble, p. 31; Hankins, "Lear and the Psalmist."

and never wrong. He alludes to a passage from Scripture which supports what he says, though it states the reverse of what he believed before his tragic exposure. "Yea God is faithful, for our preaching to you, was not yea and nay. For Gods sonne Jesus Christ, which was preached among you by us, even by me and Silvanus, and Timotheus, was not yea and nay, but in him it was yea" (II Cor. 1:18, 19). Against the background of the Bible the passage emphasizes Lear's common humanity and his realization of it by contrasting his flatterers with Christ's followers and by contrasting himself with the Christ who could speak peace to the storm (Mark 4:39) while the thunder does not heed Lear's bidding.

The one person, besides Kent, who did not "yea" and "nay" Lear was Cordelia. He realizes, at last, that she has really loved him. His realization comes like that of the prodigal son. Cordelia says,

> and wast thou fain, poor father,
> To hovel thee with swine and rogues forlorn
> In short and musty straw? Alack, alack!　(IV.vii.37-40)

Cordelia's words constitute a particularly moving reversal: the father becomes the prodigal son who, after wasting his substance, "would fain have filled his belly with the cods that the swine did eat: and no man gave into him" (Luke 15:16); the daughter becomes the father who "had compassion, and ran, and fell on his neck and kissed him" (Luke 15:20).

Thus reunited with Cordelia, Lear says,

> He that parts us shall bring a brand from heaven,
> And fire us hence like foxes. Wipe thine eyes;
> The good-years shall devour them, flesh and fell,
> Ere they shall make us weep. We'll see 'em starv'd first.
> 　　　　　　　　　　　　　　　　　　(V.iii.22-25)

Lear's words allude to the story of Samson, who "caught three hundred foxes, and tooke firebrandes, and turned them taile to taile, and put a firebrande in the middes betweene two tailes" (Judg. 15:4-5) to burn up the grainfields of the Philistines. He also alludes to the dream of Pharaoh, in which "seven good kine" representing "seven good yeeres" were devoured by seven withered ears "blasted with the easte winde" (Gen. 41:26). As would be expected, the passages are distorted and upside-down in Lear's madness, but, even so, the closeness between himself and Cordelia and his determination that his enemies shall not triumph over him are intensified. The Scrip-

75

tural withered years of famine, representing Goneril and Regan, shall be starved and devoured by the good years of plenty before Lear and Cordelia will weep, now that they are reunited.[32]

Pushing almost unbearably beyond this effect even, Shakespeare brings Lear and Cordelia together on the stage again. Cordelia is dead and Lear soon joins her in death. "And my poor fool is hang'd!" If an earlier allusion is remembered, the word "fool" from the confused mind of Lear has the effect of meaning the opposite of "fool" by stressing Cordelia's faithfulness and wisdom.[33] She it was who initiated the tragic action because she could not heave her heart into her mouth, for "the hart of fooles is in their mouth: but the mouth of the wise is in their hart" (Ecclus. 21:26).

32. See Kenneth Muir (ed.), *The Arden Edition of the Works of William Shakespeare: King Lear* (Cambridge, Mass., 1952), p. 201n24. Muir cites the Biblical passage but precedes it by examples of the *NED* definition of *Goodyear*, "used in imprecatory phrases as denoting some undefined malefic power." For an argument in favor of James 5:2-3 as the text for Lear's "commentary on the transitoriness of worldly goods," see Elton, "Lear's 'Good Years'"; his point is that both "fire" and the eating of "flesh" by riches appear in James. Since in Lear's speech, "fire" is connected with "foxes," however, I believe the meaning of the passage is that given in the text above.

33. See Stroup, "Cordelia and the Fool"; proposing further arguments and more evidence for the theory that the parts of Cordelia and the Fool were written for the same boy actor, Stroup's thesis perhaps reinforces the evidence of Biblical allusion cited above for Shakespeare's intentional association of Cordelia and the Fool in the audience's mind as well as in Lear's. Nor is the association "confused" as Bradley suggests in *Shakespearean Tragedy* (New York, 1957), p. 251.

CONCLUSION

I have presented here a sampling of dramatic uses of Biblical allusion in English drama, particularly in the plays of Marlowe and Shakespeare. The treatment has been intended not as exhaustive but as illustrative of the multitude of ways these dramatists found to add depth and breadth to the effectiveness of their characterization, dialogue, foreshadowing, irony, and to the total working out of theme by depending on knowledge already in the minds of the audience (and, therefore, needing no exposition)—knowledge of the stories, characters, and allegorical and doctrinal interpretations of the Bible. There remains a wealth of further illustrations of the same patterns of allusion, quotation, paraphrase, and idiomatic echo that I have pointed out, indeed of further patterns. But I have sought to substitute careful selection for the indiscriminate multiplication of examples.

Many important questions remain to be answered; each reader has doubtless made his own checklist, mentally at any rate. Is there a correlation between the frequency of Biblical allusions and the dates of the plays? Is Shakespeare's ability to use classical and topical allusions comparable to his ability to use Biblical allusions? Does Shakespeare limit his use of certain Biblical references to certain types of dramatic character? And so on. My aim has not been to answer, or even to anticipate, all such questions; rather, it has been to answer one major question: Is there a discernible continuity in the uses made by English dramatists of Biblical allusion, especially from Marlowe to Shakespeare? The answer is yes. Shakespeare's mastery in the use of the Bible for dramatic effect is not an independently constructed, disconnected mansion. Modified and perfected as his patterns are, one can discern still the outlines of the patterns of his predecessors, particularly Marlowe. As readers, our alertness should be considerably increased by the evidence of his deliberate reinforcement and extension of that art by his appeal to, sometimes even dependence upon, the Biblical knowledge of his audience to enable them to grasp more fully the meaning of his plays.

BIBLIOGRAPHY

BIBLES

The Bible and Holy Scriptures, Conteyned in the olde and newe Testament. Translated according to the Ebrue and Greke and conferred With the best translations in divers languages. Geneva. Printed by Rowland Hill, MDLX.

Biblia Sacra. Vulgate Editionis, Sixti V. et Clementis VIII. Londoni: Sumptibus Samuelis Bagster, n.d.

The Holie Bible. Conteyning the Old Testament and the new: newly translated out of the Originall tongues: & with the former translations diligently compared and revised by his Maiesties special Commandement. Appointed to be read in the Churches. Imprinted at London by Robert Barker, Printer to the Kings most Excellent Maiestie, Anno Dom. 1612.

The Holie Bible. Imprinted at London in Powles Churcheyarde By Richard Iugge, Printer to the Queenes Maiestie. 1572. (Bishops' Bible).

EDITIONS OF PLAYWRIGHTS

Brooke, C. F. Tucker (ed.). *The Works of Christopher Marlowe*. Oxford: Clarendon Press, 1925.

Brooke, C. F. Tucker, and Nathaniel Burton Paradise (eds.). *English Drama: 1580-1642*. Boston: D. C. Heath and Co., 1933.

Neilson, William Allan, and Charles Jarvis Hill (eds.). *The Complete Plays and Poems of William Shakespeare*. New York: Houghton Mifflin Co., 1942. (The New Cambridge Edition; line-numbering of the *Globe* ed.)

Wright, Thomas (ed.). *The Chester Plays*, 2 vols. in 1. London: The Shakespeare Society, 1843.

BOOKS AND ARTICLES

Ackermann, Carl. *The Bible in Shakespeare*. Columbus, Ohio: Lutheran Book Concern, 1936.

Anders, H. R. D. *Shakespeare's Books: A Dissertation on Shakespeare's Reading and the Immediate Sources of His Works*. Berlin: G. Reimer, 1904.

Barnet, Sylvan. "Some Limitations of a Christian Approach to Shakespeare," *ELH*, XXII (1955), 81-92.

Battenhouse, Roy W. *Marlowe's Tamburlaine: A Study in Renaissance Moral Philosophy*. Nashville, Tenn.: Vanderbilt University Press, 1964.

————. "*Measure for Measure* and the Christian Doctrine of the Atonement," *PMLA*, LXI (1946), 1029-59.

Bethell, S. L. "Shakespeare's Imagery: The Diabolic Images in *Othello*," *Shakespeare Survey*, V (1952), 62-80.

Bowden, Henry Sebastian. *The Religion of Shakespeare: Chiefly from the Writings of the Late Mr. Richard Simpson*. London: Burns & Oates, 1899.

Bowers, Fredson. "Death in Victory," *South Atlantic Bulletin*, XXX (March, 1965), 1-7.

————. "Dramatic Structure and Criticism: Plot in *Hamlet*," in *Shakespeare 400*, ed. James G. McManaway. New York: Holt, Rinehart and Winston, 1964.

————. "Hamlet as Minister and Scourge," *PMLA*, LXX (1955), 740-49.

———— "The Moment of Final Suspense in Hamlet: We Defy Augury," in *Shakespeare Commemorative Volume*, ed. Edward Bloom. Providence: Brown University Press, 1963.

Brockbank, J. P. *Marlowe: Dr. Faustus.* London: Edward Arnold, 1962.

Brooke, Nicholas. "Marlowe as Provocative Agent in Shakespeare's Early Plays," *Shakespeare Survey,* XIV (1961), 34-44.

Brooks, Harold F. "Two Clowns in a Comedy (to say nothing of the Dog): Speed, Launce (and Crab) in 'The Two Gentlemen of Verona,'" *English Association Essays,* XVI (1963), 91-100.

Bryant, J. A., Jr. *Hippolyta's View: Some Christian Aspects of Shakespeare's Plays.* Lexington: University of Kentucky Press, 1961.

Bullock, Charles. *Shakspeare's Debt to the Bible: With Memorial Illustrations.* London: "Hand and Heart" Publishers, 1879(?).

Burgess, William. *The Bible in Shakspeare: A Study of the Relation of the Works of William Shakspeare to the Bible with Numerous Parallel Passages, Quotations, References, Paraphrases, and Allusions.* Winona Lake, Ind.: Winona Publishing Co., 1903.

Campbell, Lily B. "*Doctor Faustus*: A Case of Conscience," *PMLA,* LXVII (1952), 219-39.

Carter, Thomas. *Shakespeare and Holy Scripture. With the Version He Used.* London: Hodder and Stoughton, 1905.

————. *Shakespeare, Puritan and Recusant.* London: Oliphant, Anderson & Ferrier, 1897.

Certain Sermons or Homilies, Appointed to be read in Churches, in the time of Queen Elizabeth of famous memory: and Now thought fit to be Reprinted by Authority from the KINGS most Excellent Majesty. 3 vols. in 1. London: Printed by T. R. for Samuel Mearne, His Majesties bookbinder, 1673.

Chambers, E. K. *The Mediaeval Stage,* 2 vols. Oxford: Clarendon Press, 1903.

Chew, Samuel C. *The Virtues Reconciled: An Iconographical Study.* Toronto: University of Toronto Press, 1947.

Cole, Douglas. *Suffering and Evil in the Plays of Christopher Marlowe.* Princeton: Princeton University Press, 1962.

Coleman, Hamilton. *Shakespeare and the Bible.* New York: Vantage Press, 1955.

Cunningham, J. V. *Tradition and Poetic Structure.* Denver: Alan Swallow, 1960.

Davidson, Clifford. "Doctor Faustus of Wittenberg," *SP,* LIX (1962), 514-23.

De Groot, John Henry. *The Shakespeares and "The Old Faith."* New York: King's Crown Press, 1946.

Dobrée, Bonamy. *Restoration Comedy, 1660-1720.* London: Oxford University Press, 1955.

Dodds, W. M. T. "The Character of Angelo in 'Measure for Measure,'" *MLR,* XLI (1946), 246-55.

Eaton, T. R. *Shakspeare and the Bible: Showing How Much the Great Dramatist Was Indebted to Holy Writ for His Profound Knowledge of Human Nature.* London: James Blackwood, 1860(?).

Elliott, G. R. *Dramatic Providence in Macbeth: A Study of Shakespeare's Tragic Theme of Humanity and Grace.* Princeton: Princeton University Press, 1958.

————. *Flaming Minister: A Study of Othello as Tragedy of Love and Hate.* Durham, N. C.: Duke University Press, 1953.

————. *Scourge and Minister: A Study of "Hamlet" as Tragedy of Revengefulness and Justice.* Durham, N. C.: Duke University Press, 1951.

Ellis-Fermor, U. M. *Christopher Marlowe.* London: Methuen & Co., 1927.

Elton, William. "Lear's 'Good Years,'" *MLR,* LIX (1964), 177-78.

Farnham, Willard. *The Medieval Heritage of Elizabethan Tragedy.* Berkeley: University of California Press, 1936.

79

Freeman, Arthur. "Othello's 'Base Indian': V.ii.347," *SQ*, XIII (1962), 256-57.

Fripp, Edgar Innes. *Shakespeare: Man and Artist*, 2 vols. London: Oxford University Press, 1938.

Frye, Roland Mushat. "Macbeth's Usurping Wife," *Renaissance News*, VIII (1955), 102-5.

———. *Shakespeare and Christian Doctrine*. Princeton: Princeton University Press, 1963.

Furness, Horace Howard. *A New Variorum Edition of Shakespeare: Othello*. Philadelphia: J. B. Lippincott Co., 1886.

Greg, W. W. "The Damnation of Faustus," *MLR*, XLI (1946), 97-107.

Hankins, John Erskine. *The Character of Hamlet and Other Essays*. Chapel Hill: University of North Carolina Press, 1941.

———. "Lear and the Psalmist," *MLN*, LXI (1946), 88-90.

———. *Shakespeare's Derived Imagery*. Lawrence: University of Kansas Press, 1953.

Hardison, O. B., Jr. *Christian Rite and Christian Drama in the Middle Ages: Essays in the Origin and Early History of Modern Drama*. Baltimore: Johns Hopkins Press, 1965.

Harrison, Frederick. *The Bible in Britain*. London: Thomas Nelson and Sons, 1949.

Harrison, G. B. "Distressful Bread," *SQ*, IV (1953), 105.

———. *Introducing Shakespeare*. New York: Penguin Books, 1947.

Hart, Alfred. *Shakespeare and the Homilies and Other Pieces of Research into the Elizabethan Drama*. Melbourne: Melbourne University Press, 1934.

Heist, William W. "Fulness of Bread," *SQ*, III (1952), 139-42.

Herr, Alan Fager. *The Elizabethan Sermon: a Survey and a Bibliography*. Philadelphia: n. p., 1940.

Howse, Ernest Marshall. *Spiritual Values in Shakespeare*. New York: Abingdon Press, 1955.

Hubler, Edward. "The Damnation of Othello: Some Limitations of the Christian View of the Play," *SQ*, IX (1958), 295-300.

Hunter, G. K. "The Theology of *The Jew of Malta*," *Journal of the Warburg and Courtauld Institutes*, XXVII (1964), 211-40.

Jack, Jane H. "*Macbeth*, King James, and the Bible," *ELH*, XXII (1955), 173-93.

Jorgensen, Paul A. "'Redeeming Time' in Shakespeare's *Henry IV*," *Tennessee Studies in Literature*, V (1960), 101-9.

Joseph, Sister Miriam. "*Hamlet*, A Christian Tragedy," *SP*, LIX (1962), 110-40.

Lewalski, Barbara K. "Biblical Allusion and Allegory in *The Merchant of Venice*," *SQ*, XIII (1962), 327-43.

Lewis, Wyndham. *The Lion and the Fox: The Role of the Hero in the Plays of Shakespeare*. London: Harper & Brothers, n.d.

Macht, David I. "Biblical Allusion in Shakespeare's 'The Tempest' in the Light of Hebrew Exegesis," *The Jewish Forum* (August, 1955), pp. 3-5.

McManaway, James G., (ed.). *Shakespeare 400: Essays by American Scholars on the Anniversary of the Poet's Birth*. New York: Holt, Rinehart and Winston, 1964.

Mahood, M. M. *Poetry and Humanism*. London: Jonathan Cape, 1950.

Meyer, Edward. *Machiavelli and the Elizabethan Drama* ("Litterarhistorische Forschungen," I). Weimar: Emil Felber, 1897.

Morrison, George H. *Christ in Shakespeare: Ten Addresses on Moral and Spiritual Elements in Some of the Greater Plays*. London: James Clarke & Co., 1928.

Nathan, Norman. "Balthasar, Daniel, and Portia," *N&Q*, n.s., IV (1957), 334-35.

Noble, Richmond. *Shakespeare's Biblical Knowledge and Use of the Book of Common Prayer as Exemplified in the Plays of the First Folio.* London: Society for Promoting Christian Knowledge, 1935.

Parrott, T. M. "Fulness of Bread," *SQ*, III (1952), 379-81.

Pope, Elizabeth Marie. "The Renaissance Background of *Measure for Measure*," *Shakespeare Survey*, II (1949), 66-80.

Pownall, Alfred. *Shakspere Weighed in an Even Balance.* London: Saunders, Otley, and Co., 1864.

Ribner, Irving. *Patterns in Shakespearian Tragedy.* New York: Barnes & Noble, 1960.

————. "Marlowe and Shakespeare," in *Shakespeare 400*, ed. James G. McManaway. New York: Holt, Rinehart and Winslow, 1964.

Rossiter, A. P. *Angel with Horns and Other Shakespeare Lectures*, ed. Graham Storey. London: Longmans, Green and Co., 1961.

Salter, F. M. *Mediaeval Drama in Chester.* Toronto: University of Toronto Press, 1955.

Sharpe, R. B. *Irony in the Drama: An Essay on Impersonation, Shock, and Catharsis.* Chapel Hill: University of North Carolina Press, 1959.

Siegel, Paul N. "Christianity and the Religion of Love in *Romeo and Juliet*," *SQ*, XII (1961), 371-92.

————. "The Damnation of Othello," *PMLA*, LXVIII (1953), 1059-78.

————. "Echoes of the Bible Story in *Macbeth*," *N&Q*, n.s., II (1955), 142-43.

————. *Shakespearean Tragedy and the Elizabethan Compromise.* New York: New York University Press, 1957.

Sims, James H. *The Bible in Milton's Epics.* Gainesville: University of Florida Press, 1962.

Small, Samuel A. "The Reflective Element in Falstaff," *SAB*, XIII (1938), 108-120, 131-43.

Spacks, Patricia Meyer. "Honor and Perception in *A Woman Kill'd with Kindness*," *MLQ*, XX (1959), 321-32.

Spivack, Bernard. *Shakespeare and the Allegory of Evil: The History of a Metaphor in Relation to His Major Villains.* New York: Columbia University Press, 1958.

Spurgeon, Caroline F. E. *Shakespeare's Imagery and What It Tells Us.* New York: Macmillan Co., 1935.

Stevenson, Robert. *Shakespeare's Religious Frontier.* The Hague: Martinius Nijhoff, 1958.

Strathmann, Ernest A. "The Devil Can Cite Scripture," in *Shakespeare 400*, ed. James G. McManaway. New York: Holt, Rinehart and Winston, 1964.

Stroup, Thomas B. "Cordelia and the Fool," *SQ*, XII (1961), 127-32.

Talbert, Ernest William. *Elizabethan Drama and Shakespeare's Early Plays.* Chapel Hill: University of North Carolina Press, 1963.

————. *The Problem of Order: Elizabethan Political Commonplaces and an Example of Shakespeare's Art.* Chapel Hill: University of North Carolina Press, 1962.

Tilley, Morris Palmer. *A Dictionary of the Proverbs in England in the Sixteenth and Seventeenth Centuries: A Collection of the Proverbs Found in English Literature and the Dictionaries of the Period.* Ann Arbor: University of Michigan Press, 1950.

Vyvyan, John. *Shakespeare and Platonic Beauty.* New York: Barnes & Noble, 1960.

————. *Shakespeare and the Rose of Love: A Study of the Early Plays in Relation to the Medieval Philosophy of Love.* New York: Barnes & Noble, 1961.

Walker, Marshall. *The Nature of Scientific Thought.* Englewood Cliffs, N. J.: Prentice-Hall, 1963.

Walley, Harold R. "Shakespeare's Debt to Marlowe in *Romeo and Juliet,*" *PQ,* XXI (1942), 257-67.

West, Robert H. "Iago and the Mystery of Iniquity," in *Renaissance Papers 1961,* pp. 63-69.

Whitaker, Virgil K. *Shakespeare's Use of Learning: An Inquiry into the Growth of his Mind and Art.* San Marino, Calif.: Huntington Library, 1953.

Williams, Arnold. *The Common Expositor: An Account of the Commentaries on Genesis 1527-1633.* Chapel Hill: University of North Carolina Press, 1948.

Wordsworth, Charles. *Shakspeare's Knowledge and Use of the Bible,* 4th ed. London: Eden, Pennington & Co., 1892 (1st ed., 1864).

Wilson, F. P. *Marlowe and the Early Shakespeare.* Oxford: Clarendon Press, 1953.

Young, Karl. *Drama of the Medieval Church.* Oxford: Clarendon Press, 1933.